ORLANDA COOK

Born in 1941, Orlanda Cook trained as a nurse and took a degree in Social Administration at Southampton University, before joining the Roy Hart Theatre as a founder member in 1972, and moving with them to the Cevennes in France in 1973. She worked with the group as a singer, actor and teacher of the voice until 1991, when she became director of the theatre, subsequently leaving for Paris and Brussels with her son, Max, to pursue her freelance career.

She is best known for her work in Sweden, where she was highly regarded as an effective and sensitive teacher of the voice. She worked alongside directors, actors and singers at the Dramatic Institute of Stockholm, the State and City Theatres, as well as the children's theatre, Unga Klara, and the Samiska Theatre in the north. She also worked with both professionals and students in Denmark, England, Hungary and the Middle East, particularly Lebanon and Jordan.

Shortly before her death in 2001, she had been invited to work with Palestinian refugees in Jerusalem, a project which was very dear to her heart. She had put the finishing touches to this, her first book, just before she became ill. She is much loved and missed by students of all ages and nationalities who had benefited from her sensitivity, warmth and compassion, and whose voices she had set free.

Orlanda Cook

SINGING WITH YOUR OWN VOICE

*A practical guide to awakening
and developing the hidden qualities
in your own singing voice*

A Theatre Arts Book

Routledge
Taylor & Francis Group

NEW YORK AND LONDON

NICK HERN BOOKS
London
www.nickhernbooks.co.uk

Singing with Your Own Voice

First published in Great Britain in 2004 as a paperback original by
Nick Hern Books Limited, 14 Larden Road, London W3 7ST

First published in the US and Canada in 2004 by
Routledge, 270 Madison Avenue, New York, NY 10016-0602,
by arrangement with Nick Hern Books.
Routledge is an imprint of the Taylor & Francis Group

Cover Design by Ned Hoste, 2H

Photography by Andrew Hickman

Typeset by Country Setting, Kingsdown, Kent CT14 8ES
Printed and bound in Great Britain by Biddles, King's Lynn

British Library Cataloguing Data for this book
is available from the British Library

ISBN 1 85459 612 8 (UK)

Cataloguing-in-Publication data is available
from the Library of Congress

ISBN 0 87830 182 8 (US)

FOR MAX

'I sing just to know that I'm alive.'

Nina Simone, American jazz singer
and High Priestess of Soul

CONTENTS

PROLOGUE

WHO IS THIS BOOK FOR?

This book will have something useful to offer you whether or not you have any previous experience of singing. The suggested explorations and exercises should be helpful to you whether you are a singer with experience who is seeking new inspiration or an amateur, dreaming of 'going solo' for the first time. Some people take to singing like ducks to water; it just comes naturally, and they don't even have to think how or why. They will stand up and sing solo at the drop of a hat, in any company and for an audience of any size. Others – perhaps you – have lost this facility. This book is for both kinds of singer, the beginner *and* the more experienced. If you are just starting to sing, the best way to a more confident approach is to begin by increasing your knowledge and awareness of the potential of the human voice, through study and practice. If you already sing, and have opened this book, it probably suggests that you are looking for ways to improve your performance. Perhaps you don't always get the most out of your voice, and you wonder why. Anyone who sings can benefit from learning more about how the voice works.

THE SONG-SHY ACTOR

All too often, an actor who is marvellously versatile with text, showing great vocal freedom and invention, will suddenly 'freeze up' when it comes to singing a song. It's as though s/he suddenly loses touch with their body – dropping out of character and apparently teetering on the edge of embarrassment, or even apology. The immense range and choice of colour and expression s/he pours into his/her speaking voice seems to be lacking when s/he thinks about singing. There seems to be only one sound available, and a risky one at that: one to hold on to at all costs, one that a moment's inattention will chase into the gravel pits, flatten or sharpen beyond recall, and generally 'betray' the actor's intention. If you could see it, there'd be a little balloon over the song-shy actor, saying: 'Sorry, I haven't got this quite right, but I'm not *really* a singer.' This book offers these actors, as well as dancers, teachers and all who use the voice to communicate, a new approach to singing.

PROCESS AND PRACTICE

By exploring process and practice, we will begin to see the foundations that good performances are built upon. These are skills that will not only help the professional or amateur singer, but will be of interest to all those interested in the human voice.

A COMPLETE OVERHAUL FOR A LIFETIME OF SINGING

Your voice, both speaking and singing, will change over time, losing or gaining expressiveness and tone, depending on whether or not you learn to understand and develop it. My aim is to help you develop your voice for a lifetime of singing, starting now and continuing into a tuneful old age – there are no age limits, at either end of the process! Start when you are ready, and then give your voice time, engagement, patience and a regular place in your timetable. This book does not offer tricks or short cuts – it offers you a complete overhaul of your voice, first and foremost by looking at the way you think about it. Gradually, with thought, listening and practice, your voice can become increasingly an outlet for your imagination, musicality and creativity, and your speaking and singing confidence can, and will, grow.

FINDING YOUR OWN VOICE

Often, through too hasty a training of the voice to 'perform', some singers never take the time to explore their own basic raw material. 'I have been singing for years,' said one student, 'but never until now with my own voice.' He realised he was always trying to sing 'like someone else'. If this is your experience, it might be useful to consider and search for the roots of your own voice. Imitative singing is useful only up to a point; after that, what about you? Do you want your voice to remain a copy of someone else's? Where is your voice? Your originality? Your song?

SINGING WITHOUT A MICROPHONE

I once asked a group of young singing students what was the first thing they needed in order to sing. Their immediate reply was: 'A microphone!' In this book, I hope to show that a microphone is actually the last thing you need: the first is your own mind, body, imagination and the air that surrounds you. We have fantastic natural abilities to project and amplify our voices; we need first to find and develop these abilities, and then we will be able to use microphones with far greater effectiveness, as a creative support and not as a crutch to our voices. This book helps you to build confidence through the discovery of your own, unassisted vocal powers. Later in your singing life you will learn to use amplifiers and microphones should they be necessary for you to communicate with a large and distant audience, perform along with an amplified band, or enhance your own well-explored vocal qualities.

THE WHOLE VOICE

'Voice' is physical, cultural, psychological and emotional, all at the same time. Voice methods do exist which attempt a separation, especially in teaching only the 'mechanics' of singing, but often, by the very fact of working on isolated areas, an imbalance is created – particularly between sound and feeling, which is then difficult to remedy. Textbooks on voice and singing cannot replace the attentive listening, intelligent guiding and encouraging support of a good teacher or singing group, but they can give you a clearer idea of the *kind* of teacher or singing group you need to find in order to develop. The aim of all good voice teaching should be to help you, first of all, to reveal the full spectrum of your voice, in colour, range and expression, *to yourself*, so that later you will have greater confidence when singing for others.

UNMASKING THE VOICE

As you begin to discover the full expressive singing range, in both height and depth, that your voice, and any human voice, is capable of, you will gradually understand what is meant by 'unmasking the voice'. Every voice is unique. There are as many kinds of voice as there are people who sing. The most experienced performer, as much as the most hesitant beginner, has somewhere to go, some aspect of voice or singing still to 'unmask' and develop. The gradual discovery, or rediscovery, both of the mind/body link and of the whole palette of your vocal colours, will help you learn any style of singing you eventually choose: classical, show, flamenco, blues, folk, pop-rock, country, oriental, ethnic or experimental jazz vocalisation. The process of 'unmasking' the voice – discovering all that can lie behind one seemingly 'fixed' sound – will gradually reveal to you your own natural and amazing vocal versatility.

This book aims to awaken your curiosity about
the roots of the human singing voice, and give you a thirst
to learn more about your own vocal potential.

ONE
Voice: Mind and Heart

'In all good music, feeling and intellect must go together.'
Alfred Brendel, concert pianist

ONE

Voice: Mind and Heart

Singing Who We Are

OVERVIEW

Singing, more than any other activity, has the ability to bring us totally into the present moment, with body and soul.

Why is it that so often the sounds that come out of our mouths fall short of our dreams? We may find that all is fine as long as we only sing 'in a certain way'. As soon as we try something else, our voice seems to fall apart. Our deepest wish is to be able to sing with ease, energy and expression, and to communicate intelligently and musically 'who we are'. At first we doubt our ability to sing authentically: we are not sure of our voices, believe ourselves to be getting it 'wrong', lose touch with our own energy and with the music, and feel inhibited about singing both from ourselves and for our listeners. Something that should be easy and natural has become difficult. Something has got in the way of our freedom of expression.

We have lost touch with the inner sources of inspiration, and are trapped in too many notions of how it 'ought' to be done. There no longer seems any one 'right' way to sing – since just about everything appears possible. We are influenced constantly by what we hear: brilliant and successful singers and musicians we admire; people who appear to know how it should be done; standards of excellence on stage and screen that we have assimilated from an early age, and the enormous and confusing mass of recorded vocal material that we are aware of all the time. How can we find our own voice, our own sound, in all this? Where should we begin?

A New Way to Listen
The best way to start finding your own voice is to begin listening to it in a new way. This means reviewing and even changing the way you think about voice in general, and your own voice in particular.

AN 'ACCEPTABLE' SOUND

The simple physical mechanics for producing vocal sound, whether by humans or by birds or animals, are broadly similar, and depend upon the interaction of three main structures:

1   A power base.
2   A vibrating centre.
3   A field – or fields – of resonance.

These structures will be explored in depth in Part Two.

The mechanics work in a very similar way for a canary, for example, as for a dog or a human. The difference between the dog, the canary and us, though, is that birds and animals are completely uninhibited about the sounds they make, and therefore tend not to impede the mechanics. Animals and birds, one presumes, have no hang-ups about their voices. They have no confusion or embarrassment about the range of sound that is likely to come out of their mouths, or whether it is acceptable or unacceptable, and therefore they can be whole-hearted and one hundred per cent engaged with whatever vocal messages they give out, from loud squeals of 'don't eat me!' to lyrical dawn symphonies of song. Vocal inhibition and constriction is a peculiarly human failing, due largely to confusion and a lack of confidence about what is an 'acceptable' sound – or sentiment.

INFLUENTIAL FACTORS

Suddenly, as a new singer – or even not so new – we come up against a familiar 'judge' inside our own heads, for whom the sound of our voice is 'no good' or 'not right'. This unrelenting judge represents the inescapable influences of family, culture, fashion and society. It is what we have all experienced from an early age, through our families and our peer groups, from the culture we grew up with and the society we live in. At best, these influences are stimulating, supportive, creative and encouraging. At worst, they can seriously hinder our unique vocal potential. We learn to produce the vocal sounds that are expected of us, and that 'fit in' with the environment around us.

PLACING THE VOICE

We continually try to reinforce the mental attitudes and physical movements that influence and shape the sound of our voices as they are now, much as in a similar way we work at the facial expressions we present to the outside world. In a sense, we are all highly accomplished 'technicians' in relation to our voices. We are, quite unconsciously, already 'placing' our voices, whether high or low, rough or smooth, tuneful or monotonous, soft or sharp, through a complex learned interaction of muscular activity and brain processes. We constantly adjust our voices to what we believe will be an 'acceptable' sound: that is, acceptable relative to criteria and standards that we have consciously or unconsciously accepted to be the best, or most appropriate. We try to conform to some model, which may or may not be in tune with the reality of our own voice. For instance, we might have spent years trying to sing with a beautiful pure high voice, when actually it is in the deeper range of our voice that we feel most authentic. Or we might have developed a habit of belting out every song, regardless of an inner longing to express simple warmth, or we might have shaped our voices to sound just like 'everyone else', when all the time we have been aware of hidden and special qualities longing to find expression. We seek to please not ourselves but that familiar judge, whose approval seems so important.

THE NEW AND UNKNOWN

The voice carries our identity, and we are very attached to what we know of it and what it represents in terms of self-recognition. In the process of exploration and development described in this book, some hitherto untapped or hidden vocal quality may well emerge fully formed, just as Athena was supposed to have done from Zeus's head! This can be very exciting if we are ready for such revelations, but it can also be disturbing, because the new sound can radically change our idea of who we are. 'Is this me?' is a question I have often heard from astonished students when their voice suddenly reveals itself in this way. Once released, a new sound opens up the voice, in the same way that some startling revelation can open the mind and change our way of thinking.

REVEALING THE VOICE

Exploring the voice and discovering new vocal sound is like enlarging one's wardrobe, changing costume and style, or even doing without costume at all. The idea of the 'naked' voice has a different appeal for different people. Some people might prefer to keep their voices 'fully clothed' – and indeed, why not! And yet who has not been in admiration of a singer who was able to give the impression of revealing all, of laying bare their whole soul; of being 'naked' but still in command of themselves? The ability to 'unmask' the voice is similar to that required by an actor who plays with a multitude of different masks, able eventually to assume, or discard, any mask or expression according to the artistic demands of the situation, the music and the text.

CREATING NEW HABITS

When we begin to seek qualities of sound that are different from those we habitually make, we have to work hard to bring about the changes. We have to undo habits in the muscular behaviour of our bodies so that we can 'place' and direct our breath differently, and begin to allow our voices to rediscover the natural springs of energy and expression. Singing, much more than speaking, requires an awareness of what is happening on a physical and emotional level, inside the head and inside the body.

It is important to remember that attempts to break through any established patterns of muscular behaviour without really appreciating that we, together with the influences surrounding us, set them up in the first place can, and actually does, result in physical symptoms, such as headaches or muscular constriction, particularly in the throat.

We have to be in agreement with changes to our habitual vocal sound and have a mental concept of what we are moving towards – and, more importantly, expand our idea of the possible. The more we develop this mindset, the stronger the mental image, the clearer the body signals and the clearer the sound.

WHOSE VOICE IS IT?

The very way we talk about the voice defines it and shapes it. We say things such as: 'My voice doesn't obey me', and 'I want to be able to control my voice', as though our own voices were some sort of other being or appendage, or an unruly and uncontrollable substance or animal. We are afraid our voice will 'betray' us or 'let us down'. Maybe if we couldn't see or feel our own bodies, we might insist on our elbows behaving like feet – and suffer just the same anxieties when they didn't! Once we have discovered the full possibilities of our voices, in range, colour and expression, we will begin to make reasonable demands and possibly begin to feel less 'let down' and more fulfilled. It might be useful to review the whole notion of 'obedience and control', starting with the voice.

THE INSTRUMENTAL VOICE

The eminent conductor Sir Henry Wood recommended that 'for the first three years, singers should be trained to make their voices like *a beautiful even instrument*' (my italics). Voice training, as practised in classical music colleges, links vocal development immediately to a particular musical aesthetic. You are encouraged to think of your voice as a musical instrument, in order to develop it appropriately. If, on the other hand, you consider your voice as a personal expression of your innermost being, you will immediately have another kind of relationship to your voice, less instrumental and more human. We have to ask ourselves '*who* is playing the instrument?' You may learn that your voice can be both instrumental *and* a full expression of who you are. Both concepts influence your attitude and your ability to discover the full range of your voice.

Picturing the Voice
How would you describe your own voice to yourself?
What words would you use? If you could draw a picture
of your voice, how would you draw it, and how many
different colours would you use?

The Natural Voice

Is there really such a thing as the 'natural voice'? Is it the same for everyone – and how can we recognise it? And if there is, is it the one we would really want? What are the attributes and qualities of such a voice? The following section seeks to explore this question, which is crucial to the mental attitudes you bring to your own vocal explorations and to the full development of your vocal powers.

BORN NOISY

We tend to forget that, like other mammals of the natural world, we are born not as the quiet, well-behaved, civilised beings we are now, but as noisy creatures! We are born with the ability to 'give voice' as and when necessary for survival. The laryngeal tract within the throat, designed principally to protect our airways and stop us from choking, also contains structures that specifically enable us to create loud, penetrating or appealing sounds when necessary. Anyone with recent experience of small babies will know this intimately. We can scream and yell and wail without any prompting and without the slightest need for having heard any such sounds before. Our first sounds are truly authentic, and as natural to us as coughing and sneezing – and probably just as closely related to immediate stimuli. We are, with some exceptions, noisy, communicative and vocal. Even without words, the very young child is able, if necessary, to maintain a constant stream of vocal communication with the outside world. Not: 'I think, therefore I am', but: 'I give voice, therefore I am'.

A GOOD START

Since voice is all about communication, we soon learn to modify our cries to suit our family and social environment and to achieve our aims of being loved and accepted – or at least taken care of! The urge to use the voice appropriately is a strong one: our very survival depends on it. If we achieve our aims by eventually learning to be quiet, then we will be quiet. If our boisterous outpourings, as well as our tender mewlings, are understood and accepted, then we stand a good chance of developing strong flexible voices rich in texture, feeling and expression.

MOTIVATIONS, MESSAGES AND SIGNALS

Vocalising of every kind is an integral and important part of our infant state. Imagine any young child, chuckling when happy, screaming when thwarted, crying noisily when hurt or enraged, then humming or chanting when once again comforted and happily occupied. As infants, our voices were totally responsive and linked to our needs, appetites, moods and attempts at socialising – we owned a voice free from cultural or linguistic conditioning, a voice entranced by its own magic power. We all had the innate ability to express immediately and wordlessly every shade of feeling known to us. Our communication was clearly linked to motivation; we gave out vocal messages and signals to increase our sense of security or pleasure – it was the content of our message that determined the *pitch* of sound we used.

Early Memories

Can you bring to mind any specific moment when, as a child, you felt the full power or magic of your voice, or of another person's voice? Were you personally encouraged – or hushed? Early memories of our own vocalising or singing, and the sounds or music we heard, have the power to reconnect us to forgotten sources of energy and pleasure.

THE IMPORTANCE OF LISTENING

'If we had a keen vision and feeling of all ordinary human life, it would be like hearing the grass grow and the squirrel's heart beat, and we should die of that roar which lies on the other side of silence.'
George Eliot, *Middlemarch*, 1871-2

A great deal of our present vocal ability is dependent on what we have heard, especially of a musical or vocal nature, going on around us. The bones of the inner ear are the same size for us as adults as for when we were newborn. This means that as babies we have immense powers of aural perception. At the beginning of life, we are more open to every sound that surrounds us than ever again. 'By the age of ten we've heard as great a range of sound as we'll hear for the rest of our lives' (*The Human Body*, BBC, 1998).

Dr Alfred Tomatis, the highly-respected French researcher on voice and hearing, said that we do not sing with our mouths but with our ears and our brains. Our perceptions of the sounds we hear determine everything. We are a part of what we hear, or what we don't hear. We learn to select from that 'roar' of sound, whether we perceive it consciously or unconsciously. This necessarily selective process of listening results in much of what we hear falling into unconscious memory; memories that in later life will feed, or impede, the musical imagination and even vocal ability. It is worthwhile taking some time for reflection, for letting the musical and auditory memories re-surface, even for writing them down or telling them – you may find within them all sorts of clues to your own natural singing ability and potential now. For example, if you grew up either by the sea,

in the depths of the countryside, or in the centre of a busy metropolis, the daily 'soundscape' that surrounded you would be qualitatively different for each.

The sea creates ever-changing yet familiar sound patterns; the countryside provides silence as a background to sound; cities offer increasingly dense 'soundscapes', with few moments of silence but with an exciting and stimulating variety of noise. You may have grown up in the city, yet longed for the holidays that took you to different landscapes and different sounds. You may have been surrounded by mainly man-made sounds, or by natural ones. It matters whether our first burblings were accompanied by the sound of seagulls, crows, nightingales or city sirens! The music you listened to might have been an intrusion from noisy neighbours, or music you were able to choose and listen to in peace and quiet – and turn off when you wanted. You may have grown up in the midst of a noisy and vocal family, or in a quiet and restrained one, where loud voices and even singing were rare events. Can you remember any moments when you suddenly became aware of the very act of listening?

NATURAL IMITATORS

As a species, we have an instinctive capacity, closely linked to our hearing and listening abilities, to imitate. As babies and young children, we are particularly good at reproducing those sounds that will bring us into closer communication

21

with those we depend on or wish to attract, in order to gain love and approval. We train our own voices from the very start! Laryngologist Tom Harris says: 'We are all international concert pianists with our vocal folds' (*A History of the Voice*, BBC Radio 4, 2000). We have an amazing natural ability, as a result of the ear/voice/brain connection, to pick up and reproduce new sounds, through extremely accurate muscular adjustments within the larynx (see more in Part Two). So extremely delicate are the adjustments that they allow us to make our voices 'the same but different'. We develop the social sounds we need, and keep that essentially personal sound which enables immediate vocal recognition and identification.

BIRDS, BEASTS AND BABIES

The imitative skill is part of the amazing and complex process through which our maternal language is so rapidly and efficiently learned. This skill arises as much from the ability to control the muscles of speech as from a playful approach to practice. If you once found the muscular control and mental concentration needed in order to learn speech, you can find it again in order to pick up a song. The young child will playfully repeat many times a new sound or tune picked up from the family or close environment, until it is perfected, much as s/he learns to speak. No boring scales here! Birds, in a similar way, repeat, perfect and develop their calls and songs over a period of years. We wonder why our musical skills so often lag behind the spoken ones – they would be equal if, like birds training a new call, or small children learning to speak, we practised and repeated out loud the difficult bits all the time!

EXPANDING THE VOICE

Birds expand their repertoire of song by imitating human sounds, just as we humans once used to enrich our own singing through imitations of birds and animals. In the past, and even today, where animal and human worlds are more closely linked, many singing traditions throughout the world have been inspired directly by the sounds of animal calls and cries, giving a wide vocal spectrum. The essence of Nordic Sami singing, for instance, is derived from animal and bird calls of all kinds, including fox calls and reindeer sounds, and Hindu singing, even though highly stylised, is full of direct references to animal voices. The human desire to imitate birdsong probably inspired the creation of one of the first known musical instruments, the reed pipe or flute.

One of the greatest compliments that could be paid to a woman's (and some-times a man's) singing voice in the past – and still today, in certain cultures – was to compare it with either a bird or a flute. This tendency we have as a species to 'pick up', play with and imitate different kinds of sound enriches and expands our vocal range and quality. It reveals something important about the development of our innate vocal capacity, and demonstrates a real need for outside stimuli or sources of inspiration.

Practice Makes Perfect
In producing and playing with any new and fascinating sound, the child pleasurably and effortlessly develops and exercises the vocal muscles that will enable him/her to continue further singing activity in the future.

NEEDS AND MOTIVATIONS

The only other creature in the world that has anything approaching the imitative ability of humans is the Australian lyre bird, as David Attenborough observed in *The Life of Birds* (1998). This bird uses its highly-skilled and varied repertoire of imitations (including sounds of mechanical chain saws overheard in its native forest) as part of an elaborate courtship song and dance. The sounds it makes clearly represent signals, messages and motivations. Similarly, all human sound, whether we recognise it or not, is linked to a conscious or unconscious message. As singers we need to gradually give recognition to the 'content' of vocal sound. Do we try to sing the highest note in our vocal register to show how gifted we are, to prove our strength, to attract attention or to heighten emotion? What messages, signals or motivations are we expressing, or do we wish to express, through song?

DISGUISING THE VOICE

As a species, we have, through the voice alone, a natural ability to assume and create a huge range of roles and identities, both human and animal, for the purposes of play, communication or ritual. The origin of this imitative vocal skill was probably not to win in certain kinds of singing contest, but was probably much more serious, relating to the need to catch or tame wild prey. Many adults in voice and theatre improvisation workshops show an ability to make amazingly lifelike imitations of wild animal and bird sounds, without apparently having had any real contact with the wild. Given the opportunity and the right setting, students can howl like wolves, hoot like owls, crow like cockerels, scream like baboons, bleat like sheep, bray like donkeys and even, if required, sing as lyrically as birds or dolphins. This extraordinary ability seems to suggest something that goes deeper than just imitative skill.

REAL OR FAKE?

The making of these animal-like sounds, which appear strangely authentic for the person who voices them, evoke what might be called a genetic memory from our evolutionary past. They are not imitations, but are part of the vocabulary of sounds once banned from civilised speech and behaviour, the 'forbidden sounds', savage and devilish, that once sent a shudder down the civilised spine – they represent the hidden, primitive and 'natural' part of our own human voices.

'We are Stone Age bodies in a highly technological world.'
The Human Body, BBC, 1998

First Voices

A few important facts:

1   Genetic research reveals that the difference between our chromosomes and those of our ape ancestors is only two per cent. It is that vital two per cent which gives us the physical ability to develop speech as we know it. The remaining ninety-eight per cent links us to the world of all other mammals.

2   As a species, we began to develop speech only about 150,000 years ago. This development was linked to the lengthening of the human neck. If you stretch out the back of your neck you will see that your speech will be clearer than if you speak from a cramped and hunched position!

3   Our primitive ancestors had the same physical and vocal capacities – and potential – as we have now.

MEANINGFUL UTTERANCES

As infants – in other words 'young mammals', not yet civilised – we develop, like the higher primates such as chimpanzees, a highly expressive vocabulary of

vocal sounds to communicate our needs. Even with the development of speech, these sounds can remain part of our language for a long time, especially when urgent and immediate vocal communication is required. Every teacher is familiar with the sounds of young children reverting to animal-like cries in play. Screeches, squeals and squawks, like those of parrots or monkeys, come to them more easily and more effectively than speech in moments of teasing and taunting, and release a fuller range of the voice than speech allows. The vocal muscles are exercised by these moments of freedom from speech, and the energetic link with the whole body is renewed.

As we shall see later, we can re-create such moments with the aim of re-establishing an energetic link through voice and body. (See in Part Two: PVE, Laughter and the Jaw, page 57.)

PRIMITIVE VOCAL ENERGY: PVE

The real power supply of the voice, the one that gives us the ability to harness the full potential of its power and expression, is our attitude towards Primitive Vocal Energy, or, as I will call it from now on: 'PVE'. PVE is wordless vocal expression that bypasses the rational part of the brain. It reveals itself in our immediate vocal response to a situation or feeling. It is that other part of our voice, neither spoken nor sung, that erupts out of our conscious control in exclamations, shouts, hoots, screeches, guffaws, roars, whoops, chuckles, yells, calls, laughter and cries. It is the very personal range of *non-verbal* sound we are capable of making, both loud and not so loud, often quite unconsciously, for a multitude of reasons, in the course of a normal day.

RAW MATERIAL FOR SONG

You could imagine non-verbal sounds as being the raw material of the voice. They have the power to tell you a great deal about your whole voice spectrum. A wordless exclamation of complete surprise and amazement, or a peal of laughter, can lead you into a higher range of your voice than you would have thought possible. A relaxed and rumbling belly laugh can make you aware of the lower range of your voice, and sudden shouting or yelling can tell you more than you would perhaps like to believe about your ability to project your voice – like barking! Pre-verbal vocalising, as well as acting as a kind of emotional safety valve, also enables us to reach and exercise parts of the whole voice spectrum that lie well beyond the range of most simple songs. As we bring such expression into our conscious awareness, it will begin to enrich and invigorate our singing and speaking voices.

A NATURAL SOURCE OF VOCAL ENERGY

Observing and exploring this natural source of vocal energy can lead you to explore higher and lower ranges of vocal sound, and increased resonance, without worrying about 'getting it right'. If you can reach high, middle and low sounds through expressions of PVE, you will eventually be able to find and develop your singing sound with this same range. Ask yourself how you feel about this area of your voice. Are you happy that your voice sometimes bursts out of your conscious control? How much attention or conscious awareness do you give to your expressions of PVE? Listen to your laughter, observe the sound of your own anger or exasperation.

HEALTHY VOICES

The healthy development of resonance and vibrancy in the singing and speaking voice depends largely on allowing time for the natural channelling of PVE during infancy – in other words, on allowing kids to shriek! When this is not allowed to happen, for whatever reason, energy is gradually removed from the speaking and singing voice, and remains as a repressed source of energy. Students with difficulties in making loud sounds, or finding expressiveness in the voice, have sometimes told me they were constantly hushed as children. PVE (Primitive Vocal Energy), with its direct link to energy and feeling, needs to be recognised and re-integrated as part of the source material of the singing voice.

An interviewer once asked Pavarotti, 'Would you consider some of the sounds you make as being, er, rather primitive?' Pavarotti replied, 'Non primitivi! Animali!'

The Singing Voice

Have you noticed how often small children sing wherever they happen to be, whether they are at home, in the school playground, on the bus, in the shops or with their toys? They laugh, then maybe they wail and cry, then they chatter or sing again – vocal sound serving as a barometer of their state of being. They sing, chatter or shriek whatever words happen to be uppermost, playing with sound, tone and speech; they practise, ad infinitum, words, sounds and whole phrases, sometimes stringing them all along on one highly individual, improvised, melodic and clear 'tone-flow'.

The singing sound, of whatever quality, is essentially a vocal sound that can be sustained.

The song-like cattle call of certain indigenous peoples is acknowledged to have grown out of the ability to sustain and sing out a call or cry. Any sound at all that can be sustained turns into a kind of singing. Think of the difference between a dog barking and a dog howling, or the staccato-like quality of laughing and the sing-song sound of wailing. One sound is a series of short vocalisations, as in speech; the other is sustained, as in singing. Singing is sometimes described as 'sustained talking on a tune'. It is a very small step from speech into song, almost as though song is 'hovering' there all the time. Try speak–singing a phrase or sentence from the newspaper, or this book, and notice how easily you fall into a kind of chanting.

> *'I sing because I'm happy, I sing because I'm free.'*
> Civilla D. Martin, 'His Eye is on the Sparrow', 1905

The 'singing sound', which may be tiny and fragile, has been frequently ob-served in young babies from as early as six months or even earlier. This suggests that it is not a vocal skill we have to learn, like speech, but more like something that could be called 'instinctive'. The singing sound as it first emerges in the very young is yet another wordless communication linked directly to the feeling state – in this sense it is also at root a primitive sound. It is an expression of well-being, pleasure or contentment. Suddenly the baby discovers a sound that requires no answer, that is an answer in itself. The child plays with this sound, gurgling and listening to itself. A new kind of communication and listening is established, as much inward as outward. Probably the most unique and important moment in our entire development, whether observed or not, comes through the emergence of that first frail singing sound.

DO BE, DO BE, DO BE, DO BE

There is something important to learn about singing from that moment when 'being' takes over from 'doing'. It is this amazing change in our relationship to our voices that we have to rediscover when as adults we search for the magic of the singing sound. We have to find the ability to 'let something happen' without forcing it to happen – to allow the smallest, softest sounds to flow out on the breath close to the heartbeat, and to listen to them with wonder, much as we did in the infant state. We have to learn again to 'follow the sound', rather than striving to control it. When we rediscover that early connection it is like discovering the hidden source of all singing, as important a part of the total voice spectrum as the loud, brilliant and message-filled sounds of PVE.

LEARNING TO FORGET

Quite early on in our lives, another very important phase occurs: we develop the ability to separate feeling from sound. We can, for example, say the word 'hot' without actually feeling any heat. We learn to abstract and to dissociate. Next, we learn to say one thing and mean another. We play with the effect of words, we hide our thoughts and we cover our feelings. This ability to create a distance – to feel without giving direct vocal expression to our feelings, has the undeni-ably useful function of enabling us to use language as a tool to communicate information and ideas dispassionately. However, as well as replacing most raw expressions of PVE, speech can also lead us not only to mask our feelings but even to forget about the physical pleasure of the singing sound.

Have you noticed that expressions of feeling or emotion generally tend to break out of the normal speaking range of sound into either cries or whispers – or song?

THE GOLDEN AGE OF VOICE

There is a period in our life, up to about the age of six or eight years, when all aspects of the vocal spectrum are still allowed their full expression – a kind of 'golden age' of voice.

- We have learned to use speech.
- We still give voice to PVE without inhibition.
- We sing with a natural and free musicality.

From about the age of seven years onwards, the non-verbal part of vocal expression tends to be met with stronger and stronger adult disapproval – or at least less and less tolerance. During the same period, for most of us singing is largely neglected in favour of speech, out of all proportion to the other modes of vocal expression. By late adolescence or early adulthood, most of us have become verbally adept and musically silent, and we have learned to reserve non-verbal vocalising as a mainly unconscious form of self-expression, for football games and other sports events, fairgrounds, parties and pop concerts.

PARADISE LOST

Psychology recognises that the move away from our free and infant modes of communication – that 'golden age' – may not always be experienced as a happy or comfortable one. Within any group of culturally similar people, speech tends towards uniformity of vocal sound. The achievement of that similar sound is recognised as an important part of social bonding. The singing sound, on the other hand, tends towards the development of individuality, urging us towards that moment of standing alone and being listened to. Singing is recognised as being one of the last freedoms, and is always used whenever freedom or the longing for freedom needs expression. There may be times when the deep need to sing springs from a desire for freedom *from* speech!

Singing, together with spontaneous expressions of PVE, puts us back in touch with the 'golden age' of voice, in which we exercise fully the muscles of vocalising, and give expression to every aspect of the vocal spectrum.

The Individual Voice

'Musicals, you know – it's all about 'My Big Voice',
and what is all that about, hey?'
Imelda Staunton in performance
at the Donmar Warehouse, London, 1998

Having come this far, you will already be more able to accept and (hopefully) begin to welcome the wild as well as the beautiful in your unique and natural voice. But you still want to know: How high? How low? How BIG is my voice? And more importantly, where, if any, are its limits?

The twentieth century saw an exciting rebirth of interest in the 'natural' voice in all its colours, but even in the third millennium we can still be deeply influenced, and perhaps actually inhibited, by culturally ingrained ideas about the natural limitations of our own voice. 'Yes, but I'm a man and I can't sing that high!' 'Yes, but I'm a girl and I can't sing that low!' Any number of reasons, and as many fears, reveal themselves around this question: what is the span, or range, of the natural voice?

CROSSING THE 'GREAT DIVIDE'
MALE AND FEMALE VOICES

The musical conventions with which most of us are familiar divide vocal sound into 'male' voices and 'female' voices; these were introduced into our Western tradition of harmonic music about six centuries ago. These divisions are as follows:

- For men – from low to high voice: Bass, Baritone, Tenor and Counter-tenor.

- For women – from low to high voice: Contralto, Mezzo-soprano and Soprano.

Gender, as well as voice, was once clearly defined by these separate categories. This was understood to mean that men had, and ought to have, low voices – and women had, and ought to have, high voices. If a man sang with the higher part of his voice he was called a 'falsetto', or 'false soprano'. Real sopranos were female. A female 'baritone' would have been ridiculous. Women who naturally sang with the deep, husky 'male' part of their own voices would only find an audience as fairground freaks. All deep voices were, by definition, masculine, and high voices were by definition feminine, even if they belonged to a man. The deeper the voice, the more 'masculine' the owner, whether man or woman, and the higher and lighter the voice, the more 'feminine' the owner. We would say, derogatively, that a man singing with the higher part of his voice was 'effeminate' and a woman singing with the lower part of hers was 'butch'. Very few singers ever ventured across what may be called the 'great divide' between male and female voices, even if they were able to.

THE HUMAN VOICE

Today, a person's masculinity or femininity is no longer questioned or threatened by the ability to sing higher or lower than each gender is supposed to do, or be able to do. Folk song, jazz, blues, gospel, popular and ethnic singing have made us familiar with the sound of women singing with the deeper part of their voices. We are quite used to hearing men reaching well into the higher ranges of their voices, both in classical and in pop music. Both men and women sing into areas that were once considered the undisputed province of the other. 'Unisex' and cross-gender thinking has found a reflection in what is now acknowledged as 'the human voice', a voice no longer perceived as *exclusively* male or female in sound. We now realise that our singing range is not fixed high or low irrevocably according to gender. Women's voices may tend to be uniformly higher, men's voices uniformly lower, but the individual span may reach both high and low, and include both male and female sounds.

TOUCHING ON OPPOSITES

To venture across this 'great divide', and explore the higher or lower parts of the voice, can mean to touch on and give voice to the masculine aspect of a woman's character, or the feminine aspects of a man's character – that opposite part of ourselves which psychology recognises as being normal. It can be a great moment when we learn to express either very high or very low sounds, not as the domain of the opposite sex, but as an expression of our own human nature. By venturing over the 'great divide', the whole person can begin to express the 'whole voice' – and even more importantly each one can give recognition to whatever sounds in the voice, high or low, feel right and true, whether or not they 'ought' to be there.

BREAKING THROUGH THE SOUND BARRIER

Cross-gender thinking began to challenge deeply-ingrained, traditional approaches to life and to singing in the Western world as comparatively recently as the 1950s. This new awareness and acceptance of the full range of the human voice was vital in allowing everyone the freedom to develop their authentic voice; it developed principally from the researches and observations of Alfred Wolfsohn, a pioneer in the field of vocal studies. Alfred Wolfsohn convinced both scientific and musical experts that both men and women could be trained to sing from high to low through the entire classical ranges of bass, baritone, tenor, contralto and soprano, encompassing not just one *octave*, but many. This was so news-worthy a development that an article appeared in *Time* magazine on 19 March 1956:

> '*In London last week a new voice was making news. It belongs to pretty, pencil-slim Jennifer Johnson, 23, and its useful range is an extraordinary four octaves – or everything from bass to soprano.*'

Wolfsohn's first concern was to free his pupils from what he described as 'the fear of heights and the fear of depths', conditioned in their voices by tradition. The span of Johnson's voice was so impressive that it was suggested she might have an extra large throat or larynx, or a vocal apparatus different from the rest of us; but scientific research showed that her throat, larynx and vocal folds were completely normal for her age and gender.

People liked to console themselves with the belief that anything outside the 'normal' range (one-and-a-half to two octaves) was unnatural, and only possible because the singer was differently shaped, or better shaped or more oddly shaped than anyone else! The achievement of training every tone of four-and-a-half octaves to be 'useful' is still rare, but to sing through a similar vocal span with what is known as 'variable voice quality' is surprisingly common – though not all of it may be considered 'useful' for singing in the classical sense.

USEFUL OR USELESS SOUNDS

The idea of 'usefulness' is connected to a specific style of singing. In the classical tradition, vocal sound, as we have seen, is carefully selected and trained over many years for a particular beauty and evenness of tone, through a specified range. When you start to explore the 'human range' of your voice, every sound is 'useful' because every sound reveals a part of your whole voice spectrum. This leaves you to choose which qualities you wish to develop. There is, however, a developmental stage of the male voice that has long been considered useless – even embarrassingly useless; this is known as 'the break'.

A BREAK WITH THE PAST

In Mozart's opera *The Marriage of Figaro* (1786) there is a scene where an older man, Figaro, a manservant, singing with a deep male baritone voice, exhorts an adolescent boy, Cherubino (sung by a young woman), to leave his frivolous life and prepare himself for the life of a soldier. Until very recently, in our civilisation a man's unavoidable lot in life was to enter physically into battle. The warrior identity was nurtured. Being called up to fight for one's country required qualities of physical bravery – or at least the ability to silence softer voices in the soul, and speak up as a man!

The male voice appears to mirror the stark move from boyhood to manhood, when it is said to 'break'. It is a good moment, if battles are imminent, to weed out the higher, 'girlish' tones of a boy's voice, and affirm all that upholds and defines traditional 'masculine' qualities of protectiveness, strength, valour and assertiveness. And this is exactly what happened – and maybe still does; the deeper sounds which clearly differentiate boy from girl are welcomed, and all the high or tender sounds that can still be associated with girls or cherubs are chased away.

GETTING THE VOICE UNDER CONTROL

As we all know, even without the threat of battles the male voice does change, sometimes dramatically. The body grows and develops, and with it all the structures involved in vocalising. Muscles lengthen and thicken, and there is a significant physical change in the male vocal muscles: more so, comparatively, than those of the young female (See in Part Two: The Magic Cords, page 78). The young adolescent boy has to cope with a heavier body and longer limbs, triggering, not surprisingly, a period of 'clumsiness' in all sorts of other physical activities, as well as voicing. The vocal muscles no longer seem capable of responding to the normal signals. It can seem as though from one day to the next during this period, a familiar vocal sound can no longer be relied upon, almost as though a part of the voice has moved out of contact altogether. In this disturbing state of affairs, which can lead to embarrassment, mockery, shame or even distress, the adolescent wants to get things under control again as quickly as possible and to 'sound' normal.

LOST BOYS OR LOST VOICES?

Conforming to cultural norms of speech is something we all manage to do relatively easily, because it involves only one part of the voice – the speaking part. There is a period of transition, when the voice deepens and the piping voice of youth is forgotten. But for the adolescent who enjoyed singing as a child, things are different. Even though he may welcome the new depth of his adult voice, and look forward to singing in a new way, the 'break' can be experienced as a perplexing form of severance. Where has the high, musical voice gone? There is increasing evidence to suggest that even if it moves out of contact temporarily, it doesn't disappear and that, on the contrary, it remains as a part of the voice to be rediscovered and developed. The vocal muscles have certainly thickened and lengthened, but they are no less supple or responsive to clear, unconfused brain signals. The 'break' is psycho-social rather than physical. The range of the male voice is now known as having the potential to *increase* in range from low to high, including both the high and the new lower sounds, rather than diminish after puberty.

FROM GIRL TO WOMAN

Women, as well as men, can experience something similar to a 'break' in their voices. The female voice also changes and deepens with hormonal development as the woman matures, rather later than adolescence, and particularly so after the event of childbearing. Many women are unaware of their voice growing and deepening, and only the activity of singing can make the changes apparent, unless the woman herself is intent on maintaining a girlish tone of voice. Even in young women, something similar to the male adolescent loss of control can suddenly appear when singing from the deeper to the higher part of the voice, as though something 'flips' or 'cracks'. This is a familiar occurrence amongst all singers, not just the timid beginner.

Some singers – for instance, those in the flamenco tradition – use the 'break' to great musical and dramatic effect. The Western classical tradition tries to 'cover' it or even to eliminate it altogether (an impossible task). It is important to realise that there is nothing wrong with the voice: that the 'crack', or 'break', is entirely natural – and may even contain meanings that we have not yet discovered.

Gold in the Cracks

We often fear singing wrongly, or worry about our voice containing flaws or imperfections. Singing 'who we are' is about allowing authentic and human qualities of sound to come through and accepting what is actually there in the voice at the moment, regardless of what 'ought' to be there conventionally, according to gender. As we learn to listen to ourselves in a new way, following the sound, allowing it out, we will gradually be able to discern what we can develop as true and rich in our own voice, without imitation, realising that there is gold to be mined in the 'cracks'.

THE CHORDS OF EMOTION

'All art is about feelings, and most feelings are about love.'
Tamas Vasary, concert pianist

It is as important to give as much intelligent attention to your feelings as to your attitudes – for both, together with your muscles, contribute to the sound of your voice. We can learn to keep our feelings at a distance, as we did when learning language, but sooner or later we have to learn to know our own heart and to learn how and when to give voice to feeling.

'Feelings, along with the emotions they stem from, are not a luxury.'
Antonio R. Damasio, Professor of Neurology, Iowa College of Medicine,
Descartes' Error: Emotion, Reason and the Human Brain, 1994

All of us have noticed at one time or another how music or singing, even without a dramatic accompaniment, can unexpectedly bring tears to our eyes, or flood us with high and positive energy. There is a part of our brain function (in the limbic or 'lower' brain) that registers emotional well-being or pain, whether or not we allow it to be voiced. Control of these is exercised by specific locations in the upper cerebral cortex. Singing and vocalising often seem to short-circuit the upper brain's 'decisions', triggering emotions that may have been hidden, even from the singer himself. This is possibly because the brain centres concerned with the act of singing are situated very close to those concerned with the emotions.

GOING WITH THE FLOW

'I am violently happy because I love you.'
Björk, 'Violently Happy', 1993

Feelings are the same for everybody. We have all, as human beings, had the same feelings, to a greater or lesser degree, at one time or another. This is how we can recognise feelings, how we always know immediately and without hesitation whether a feeling expressed in song is true or 'acted'. Emotions are to do with movement, change and flow, so much so that they even provoke a change or increase in the secretion of certain bodily fluids. We talk about certain voices 'moving' us. A voice that is full of genuine feeling, to whatever degree, moves us because it is actually 'moving'. As the singer travels through the often confusing and contradictory flow of feeling, such as violent happiness, they literally move us along too. When we listen to a speaker or singer whose feelings are flowing, some of our own stifled emotions are touched, and we are moved.

STIFLING THE FEELINGS

'I can sing the singing and think the thinking,
but you're not going to catch me feeling the feeling.'
Dennis Potter, *The Singing Detective*, BBC, 1986

If you have been schooled by experience, by parents or by teachers, to control and hide most feelings, especially the extreme ones of rage, anger, frustration and jealousy, or even extreme elation, enthusiasm and joy, you will continue to be able to do this when singing. Having learned to do anything rather than 'feel the feeling', we can, quite unconsciously, channel energy away from the heart and guts and away from the body's feeling centre in the solar plexus. In the effort to keep the storm away, we will censor all feelings of vulnerability. Breathing becomes progressively lighter and shallower; the sound is restricted and comes from behind the nose, rather than being carried from the heart through an open throat. There are many unconscious strategies we use when we try to keep our own feelings out of the picture. Often it takes very little to restore the lost energy and fullness to the voice once again, and depends simply on recognising and acknowledging any 'here and now' feelings demanding our attention.

THE AIMS OF TECHNIQUE

Feeling is intimately linked to intention and meaning, without which any singing or vocalising is 'meaningless'. The spectrum of feeling, from pleasure to pain and back again, is always accompanied by what could be called an intention. Love requires giving, desperation begs to be heard, anger requires action, pain calls for attention, sorrow calls for solace and the return of happiness. When we can make the link between feeling and intention we will find the vocal sounds we are searching for – sounds which have meaning for us and for our listeners. The true aim of all voice and singing technique is to be able to communicate from the heart, through poetry and music, every shade of human feeling we know – from love to hate, friendship, jealousy, wonder, sorrow, pleasure, pain, anger, awe, tenderness, longing and all the other feelings and emotions that add up, often in a confusing way, to being alive.

'Your body is a home to your habitual emotional attitudes
and habitual thoughts. It 'holds' and is shaped by these factors.'
Olivea Dewhurst-Maddock, *The Book of Sound Therapy*, 1993

HEARTS FULL OF PASSION

Singing with the whole body offers us a way of expressing and even transform-ing our emotions actively and creatively. When we let ourselves 'feel the feelings', we can then 'hold' them, *and* share them.

> *'Moonlight and love songs, never out of date,*
> *Hearts full of passion — jealousy and hate:*
> *Woman needs man, and man must have his mate,*
> *That no one can deny.'*

Herman Hupfeld, 'As Time Goes By',
from *Casablanca*, 1942

By voicing our emotions, we can gradually learn to 'touch and contain' them, and to let them move and change. Sound and feeling, body and mind together, are the weft and the warp of the imaginative expressive voice. To work on one without taking into consideration the others would be like focusing everything on one side of a marriage. For you to make a happy 'marriage' with your voice you have to include *both* the partners.

A definition of song: 'an emotion put into words and music'.

Summary of Part One

- Vocal inhibition is largely due to a confusion and lack of confidence about what is an 'acceptable' sound.

- We were born 'noisy'. Our early utterances are completely linked to our emotional states.

- Primitive Vocal Energy (PVE) is a natural source of energy that reveals our potential for song. Singing is at root an instinctive and natural sound, linked to pleasurable feeling.

- The 'human voice' is a voice no longer perceived as exclusively male or female.

- The 'break' that occurs in male adolescence is psycho-social rather than physical.

- Feelings are not a luxury, they are a necessity – especially when we sing. They are a part of the equation that actually creates an alive or pleasing sound.

- The more we realise the breadth and potential of the human voice, the more we will be able to make the muscular efforts involved in freeing and developing our own voices – either by sudden revelations or through gradual change over time. We can then be whole-hearted and whole-minded in pursuit of the whole singing voice!

BEFORE YOU CONTINUE . . .

The following chapters offer a combination of theory, ideas to ponder on, and practical exercises. Each section of the chapter will begin with an overview, which is important for stimulating reflection and reminding you of the overall connection of each part to the whole.

This is followed by a guided practical exploration that will help you discover how physical structures and functions relate to giving voice, and how vocal techniques can be developed.

Key Words

 indicates an active exercise which involves moving, standing up or getting down onto the floor.

 indicates additional ideas and exercises for self-discovery which can be read and considered without necessarily having to move.

indicates further exercises to increase, over a period of time, your practical understanding of the physical structure explained or the activity proposed.

Finding an Exercise Space

To follow the explorations most usefully, you will need to find, clear, or make an exercise space. You need an area big enough for you to lie down and stretch out in: a clean, well-ventilated space where you won't be disturbed — preferably with a door to close behind you! At this stage, you won't need to soundproof your entire house or apartment; exercises that give support and resonance to your breath and your singing can often be practised quietly. You will discover that once you've found some of the inner spaces, you can exercise many muscles unobserved and quite silently, even while driving your car or waiting for a train — or for an audition.

Voice: Mind, Heart and . . . Body

'Where is the instrument whence the sounds flow?
And whose the magic hand that holds the bow?'

Rainer Maria Rilke, German poet

TWO

Voice: Mind, Heart and . . . Body

The body is the landscape of the mind –
the ground for all our feelings and imagination.

Activating the Body

The quality and expressiveness of the singing sound you make depends as much on feeling and imagination as on your actual physical engagement with the sound. Your voice and body need to continue their development together as they did during their 'golden age' in infancy. Your body is the 'ground' for all your feelings and thoughts – and songs. Once you know how to fill your body with breath and resonance, you will always be singing 'from the ground up', whether you are standing still, lying down, hanging upside down (it can happen!) or dancing around. The French singer known to millions simply as Barbara describes in her autobiography, *Il était un piano noir* (1996), the moment when suddenly her singing no longer allowed her to stand still. It was, she writes, as though sound moved through her entire body, forcing her to move with it, to use the space she inhabited and to go with the flow of music and feeling through her body.

Rediscovering the natural freedom to move the whole body from one's centre enables both stillness and mobility as an expression of feeling and intention. It will eventually allow even those important moments of singing while standing still to be experienced as dynamic – rather than, as so often, lifeless or numb with fright!

WHY ANATOMY?

An awareness of anatomy helps us to locate different body structures in relation to each other. It will solve simple mysteries, such as whether or not the air we breathe in does, or does not, get into the abdomen – and it tells us where the abdomen is! With a little knowledge of the major physical structures that enable you to create sound, you will have a firmer basis from which to develop your vocal powers. In the anatomical explanations that follow, a few essential but possibly unfamiliar technical terms will be included where to avoid them would over-simplify or even confuse.

41

KEY WORDS: MUSCLES, MOBILITY AND OPENNESS

Muscles, Mobility and Openness (MMO) are among the key words for this section. Memorise their initials in any order: Openness, Muscles and Mobility (OMM); or Muscles, Openness and Mobility (MOM). Choose whichever helps, and keep the words in mind as a guiding idea.

- *Muscles*   All movement requires muscular co-ordination. We create muscular action by sending precise signals, mostly without conscious thought, to particular groups of muscles, setting up neuro-muscular pathways. Most of the time, we don't have to think about any of this, but for particular activities in our lives our bodies have developed deliberate and precise pathways, so that, without thinking about it, we can thread a needle, hook a football, leap a hurdle, dance the salsa and so on. Our task is made all the easier because we can see, touch and easily locate and feel the parts of the body we want to move. When it comes to singing, an activity based as much on muscular activity as any other, things are less clear. Brain signals are sent off with the vaguest of directions, roughly equivalent to someone saying: 'er . . . open up, er, . . . in there . . . somewhere.' We know something has to open up at the back of the throat, somewhere in the chest, somewhere in the abdominal region, but what? And how? Upwards? Sideways? From back to front? From front to back? Imagine how difficult it would be if your brain signals were similarly imprecise about a simple act like lifting a cup.

- *Mobility, o*r movement, is life. It doesn't have to be wild, uncontrolled and meaningless; it can be, quite simply, a vibration at the heart of sound, a vibration coming from a mind and body alive and responsive to the moment. Mobility implies the ability to change the position of both inner and outer structures of the body – the space within the mouth, the backbone or the breathing muscles, for instance – with ease. Mobility means the facility to move any part of the body at will, to allow feeling and sound to flow through voice and body, both inwards to yourself and outwards to the listener.

- *Openness*   To encounter the full range of sound available to us we need to discover ways to open up the channels within the body to more air and more power. When your body is tense and tight from stress, your voice is unlikely to be full, resonant and warmly vibrating. When you know how to move deeper muscular structures from a position of relaxation to one of readiness, energy – and oxygen – can circulate more freely through the body, and a cycle of body/mind openness is established. This will help you open up and increase breathing and resonating spaces within the body.

MUSCULAR ACTION

All muscles have the same three basic actions, according to what we require from them.

- *Contracting, or shortening* If, for instance, you purse your lips, you are shortening and contracting the small facial muscles within and around the lips. When you smile, you relax the same muscles. If you grin madly, you are likely to stretch and lengthen the muscles.

- *Stretching, or lengthening* If you raise and stretch both arms above your head, you will feel your muscles stretching, right into your fingertips. At the same time you will be aware that other muscles, such as those around your shoulders, are contracting. Muscles work together to stretch and contract.

- *Relaxing* For instance, during rest or sleep it is well known for the lower jaw to drop open, when at last the muscles surrounding it stop stretching and contracting. Just relaxing the muscles surrounding the lower jaw can encourage relaxation, or even sleep.

We have muscles that we control voluntarily, and muscles that act involuntarily, without our control – the heart muscles, for example.

Every structure concerned with the creating of vocal sound can be influenced by a combination of thought, feeling, imagination and muscular action.

SOUND ACCOMPANIMENT FOR PHYSICAL EXERCISES

You can practise some of the physical exercises in this section with music of your choice, or you can make your own sounds, creating vocalisations to accompany them. Just as we don't need to wait to start singing until we understand our emotions better, in the same way we can start vocalising before we have a complete understanding of how it works. Eventually we learn through the very expression of sound itself. It's like learning to swim; nothing will happen until you actually get in the water. The water teaches you to swim. The making and exploring of vocal sound teaches you to sing. We need to start splashing around and taking our feet off the bottom – right from the start!

'Wade in the water, wade in the water, chillun',
God's a goin' to trouble the water!'

Traditional African-American spiritual

Explore

Swooping, sliding and having fun with sound

When you first start a physical exercise, make easy, unforced sounds, such as light sighs, groans and grumbles. They could be called 'Sgrumbles', or just 'SGG'.

- Sighs – like easy yawns.
- Groans – of the kind we all know about when we don't want to do something. Voicing these will help you shift the normal weight of inertia and lethargy that is part of our natural resistance to exercise!
- Grumbles – similar to groans, but delivered in your own personal gibberish.

These sorts of sounds, together with physical movement, help to get the 'motors' going and clear away the phlegm that tends to gather at the back of the throat. This is preferable to violent coughing. Let the phlegm in your throat gradually clear up from your 'sgrumbling' (which can take a few seconds or last over few minutes), then you can start singing a simple chorus of vowels to warm up your vocal muscles. These are the ones that tend to appear quite frequently in folk songs, probably for the very reason that they 'open' the voice. The vowels are E-I-E-I-O!

Pronounce the 'E' as 'EE' , the 'I' as 'AH-EE' and the 'O' as openly and roundly as you can.

Voice one at a time repeatedly, or in the sequence EE – AH-EE – O . . .

Take just the EEEEE – AAAHEEEE – OOOOO and let your voice slide (or even swoop!) from one to the other, from high to low – or low to high – on a light breath. It's a bit like a siren sound.

This kind of vocalising could sound a bit like 'swooping', the very thing that singers are always told not to do! 'Swooping' is when you 'miss' the note and sing up to it instead of on it. At this point it doesn't matter at all, so why not break a few rules, and just swoop for fun! Swooping can lead you into 'sliding' which is really sophisticated; the Italian musical term for it is 'glissando'.

'Swoop' first, then try singing or sliding your voice up and down a few times on either one of the three vowel sounds. Don't worry if your voice is a bit growly or crackly, if there is a bit of voice 'missing' on the way up or down, or if you do not achieve a beautiful sound; that's not the object of the exercise. Sing as lightly as you can to begin with, without pushing the sound or trying to make your voice go higher or lower than feels comfortable. Accept the sound you make now. As the muscles get stronger, your voice will fill out.

Explore

Muscles, Mobility and Openness (MMO) and Sighs, Groans and Grumbles (SGG) (10 minutes)

Here is a short exercise for you to try out MMO and SGG. This little exercise can be practised almost anywhere there is enough room to swing your arms; you can do it while either standing, walking or moving around.

- Stretch out and then contract the fingers of both hands a number of times, more and more vigorously. Shake out the fingers. Rub both hands together energetically. Get the palms of your hands hot!

- Now hold your right or left forearm lightly with the other hand. Keep your elbow against your side. Stretch the fingers and at the same time make small circles with the wrist. Make ten circles in one direction and ten in the other. Count out loud and grumble.

- Now on the same side, with the same arm, your elbow held against your side, relax your fingers and wrist and simply move your forearm up and down, letting your hand tap lightly onto your shoulder and then your thigh, six to ten times. Now across your body from side to side six times, and then round and round in circles, six to the left and six to the right from your elbow. Let your hand flop.

- Now drop your forearm, and, keeping your wrist and fingers relaxed, move your whole arm from the shoulder. Swing it backwards and forwards loosely; lift and wave the arm up and down and over your head. Feel the stretch in your ribs. Include movements in your elbow, forearm, wrist and fingers. Remember SGG (sighs, groans and grumbles) – allow yourself to yawn as much as possible, and vocalise freely.

- Now, with the same arm, loosely swing it *across* the body and back diagonally six times. This begins to engage your shoulder blade.

- When you have a feeling of your shoulder blade moving, spread out the whole arm and make snake-like movements from your fingers, wrist, forearm, elbow and shoulder to your shoulder blade. Let your arm drop, then make big sweeping movements with your arm over and round your head, engaging your back in the movement. Repeat. Allow your back to join in the movement. Twist and turn. Remember: Muscles, Mobility and Openness: MMO.

- Rest. Sit or lie down, and observe the feeling on the side of the body you have just exercised and compare it to the other. Observe your breathing. Roll over, get up and repeat the whole exercise on the other side with the other arm, systematically moving each part: fingers, wrists, elbows, shoulders up to the shoulder blades and the whole length of the back.

The action of moving the arm, shoulders and shoulder blades sets into movement the muscles surrounding the rib cage (or thorax) and increases the circulation of energy and oxygen throughout the body. This exercise will be referred to as the 'snake' and used again in other sections.

A Power Base for the Voice

'It is more difficult to stand than to move.'
Moshe Feldenkrais, *The Elusive Obvious,* 1981

The physical mechanics for producing sound depend upon a power base, a vibrating centre, and a field, or fields of resonance. The following sections will focus upon the body structures that provide the power base for the voice.

STAND UP AND SING

Something as simple as standing reveals almost as much about us as does the sound of our voices: how we 'hold' ourselves affects the sound of our songs. This is why we will benefit from exploring a structure we often put behind us, in more senses than one: the spine, or backbone.

Discover

How easier and better and deeper breathing begins with the backbone

Mobility in the backbone is central to better breathing. If the backbone is immobile and rigid, all the attendant structures related to breathing will be equally rigid, and the flow of air will be diminished. When you include the spine in your movements you enable even more movement in the chest or thorax, thus exercising one of the principal structures which will enable you to expand your in-breath. The 'snake' exercise can reveal to you the mobility, or relative immobility of your spine, as it is at the moment.

THE FIGHT AGAINST GRAVITY

The fight against gravity is definitely one to be taken lying down! To strengthen the backbone, we need to lie down and rediscover those very first movements of turning and twisting, of rotation and flexing, which built up the strong muscular casing of the spine and prepared it for the great moment of lifting and carrying our heavy heads – and, eventually, of achieving the uniquely human standing position.

Taking a look at your backbone

Can you make yourself a mental picture of the full length of your own backbone? Close your eyes and try. In a visualisation exercise during a class session, students were asked to make a drawing of how they see their backbone, regardless of what they know about it from pictures in books. We made two sets of drawings, one done 'cold' before movement, and one 'warm' after moving and exercising the body. The two 'backbones' were stunningly different. The most marked difference in the second set of drawings was that a lot of the backbones had developed heads and limbs.

THE TADPOLE'S TAIL

The spinal column, as it is often referred to, is really an extension of the head or skull. It is like a long tail that continues right down into the pelvis. It is the tadpole's tail, a longer one than it was when we were foetuses, but a tail nonetheless. Now, not unlike the frog, it has grown arms and legs and developed a basket-like structure – the thorax – to protect the heart and lungs, and another thick bony structure to protect the lower abdominal organs – the pelvis. The emphasis placed on this description is to help you make a mental picture of your own backbone in a new light, not as peripheral – 'back there' – but as completely central to every other structure attached to it.

Moving the backbone

- Move any part of your backbone and notice that another part of the body moves with it. Notice how your breathing is affected. How much movement can you make from the back *without moving your arms*?

- Move your head, and feel the amount of movement in your neck.

- Now try and move your neck *without moving your head*. Can you? Did you use your backbone to move your neck? Keep your mouth open and let yourself sigh or yawn as you move – this helps to relax your muscles.

- Now, with or without music or free vocal sounds, make movements lower down the spine, at waist level, just above the hip-bones. Move your spine backwards and forwards, from side to side and rotating sideways. This exploration may lead you into twists and turns, rollings and stretchings, through the whole body.

• Be prepared to get down to it, on the floor. Don't forget to breathe.

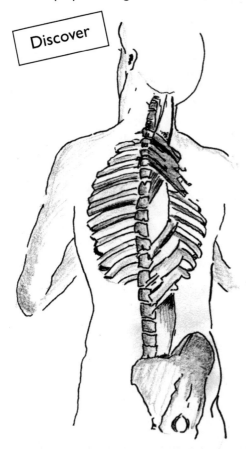

Discover

A flexible spine

We are able to twist and turn because of the structure of 24 separate and individually characteristic bones of the long spine. These are called vertebrae.

Starting from the top of the spine, there are seven vertebrae in the neck (cervical vertebrae, or cervical spine); twelve larger ones from the neck down to about the waist (dorsal vertebrae), and at the bottom of the spine five larger ones still (lumbar vertebrae). These last ones connect with the sacrum, which is in fact five fused vertebrae, about the same dimension as the palm of your hand and which articulates (is joined) with the two pelvic bones.

The spinal column functions as a structural support, and also protects the main nerve pathway from the cerebral cortex. This central nerve pathway contains a crystal clear fluid – the cerebro-spinal fluid. It is worth remembering that the backbone is actually a water channel, just as a tree-trunk is a channel for sap. Just consider for a moment how the inner substance of our spinal column is fluid, flexible and flowing – allowing maximum mobility.

SOUND CONDUCTORS

Another point to be considered here is that water, like bone, resonates sound vibrations in a particular way. Singers really *do* 'vibrate' with sound. Sound vibrations, set in motion in the vocal tract, can and do vibrate through the bony and liquid structures of the entire body, especially along the spine.

Three secret keys to flexibility, deeper breath and more resonance

Key No. 1

Place the first two fingers of both hands lightly together on the back of your neck. Tilt your head backwards; you will feel the contraction of long muscles either side of the bones of the neck. The place of 'tilt' is only possible at the 'hinge' between the third and fourth cervical vertebrae and nowhere else.

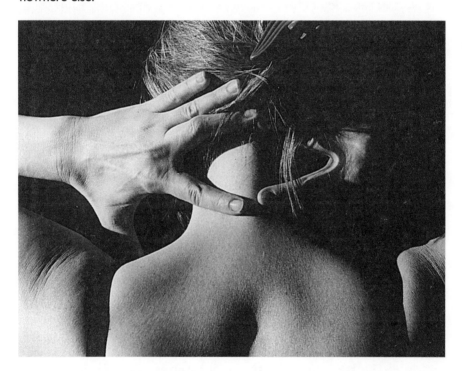

Think of this as the first 'key' to flexibility; explore the backward tilting movement. If this 'key' place is closed or compressed through a slumping posture or by jutting out your chin, your breathing will be constricted. Try some SGG with the 'key' area of your neck closed off, and then with it open. Hear the difference. Place an imaginary 'eye' over the 'tilt' joint: lengthen the back of your neck with the idea of opening the 'eye'. Do this movement without pulling in your chin towards your chest in a military way.

Key No. 2

The second 'key' is just below the shoulder blades, between the ninth and tenth dorsal vertebrae. This 'key' place allows a very small but very important upward arching of the upper back, that as a consequence opens out the rib cage in a natural and easy way. The best way to find it on your own is to sit on a chair whose back just fits comfortably below your shoulder blades, wriggle them over the edge and then arch the upper part of your back upwards. Remember to keep your seat firmly pressed against the back of the chair. If you don't have such a chair, try lifting the upper back slightly backwards and upwards, without adding extra hoisting from the shoulders. You will immediately feel an expansion in the whole of your rib cage, and the pleasant sensation of having made yourself more space to breathe.

Key No. 3

The third 'key' is that famous 'hollow' in the lower back between the fourth and fifth lumbar vertebrae, which is – and needs to be – far more mobile than you might think. It allows for forwards and backwards bending and rotation. The 'hollow' is natural, but should not be accentuated: the important thing here is mobility. Place your hands, with your thumbs meeting each other, in your back, with your fingers pointed forwards over your hip bones and around your waist. Press your thumbs quite firmly into your back and, *at the same time,* press your back into your thumbs; there should be some movement, however small, at the level of each of the five lumbar vertebrae. The lumbar spine is the 'anchor' point for the back of the diaphragm, the major muscle of respiration. The flexibility in this area, or lack of it, will affect your ability to take a 'deep' breath.

KEEPING THE CHANNELS OPEN

It is important to know that smaller nerves from the spinal column branch off between each vertebra and nourish different organs and systems of the body. The nerve pathway relaying signals from the cerebral cortex to the diaphragm separates from the spinal column at the level of the third and fourth cervical vertebrae. This is *exactly* at the 'key' point, or hinge, where we tilt our heads backwards. Awareness of this can further remind you to stretch out the back of the neck and keep the channel open. This nerve, the phrenic nerve, gives its name to words such as 'frenzy', 'frantic' and 'frenetic'. Pressure and tension in this 'key' part of the cervical spine affects both our breathing and our energy levels. A build-up of tension from hunched-up shoulders can effectively close the cervical 'key' point just as much as drooping the head and pushing the chin forwards in response to the downwards pull of gravity. Vocalising or singing freely and happily under these conditions is like trying to dance in a straitjacket!

Energy begins in the back. Mobility begins in the back.
Breathing begins in the back.

SHOCK–ABSORBERS

Each vertebra is protected from the one next to it by an inter-vertebral disc. The function of these 'cushions' is to allow mobility, to keep the space open for the nerve pathways and to absorb the many shocks our daily lives inflict upon the spinal column. These shocks range from the unnecessary jarring caused by prolonged running to the over-stretching caused by letting the heavy head hang downwards from a standing position by rolling down the back.

POINTLESS PAIN

Pointless aches or pains are the sort that come when the body is out of balance, or out of alignment. Energy used in coping with pointless pain is not free to connect with imagination and feeling in song. We have to learn to free the body as well as the voice. Experience of tension or pain in the lumbar region often comes from prolonged periods of sedentary occupation. Too much sitting tends to tip the pelvis forwards and 'close' or compress the lumbar regions at the back. Most aching in the lower back is a signal to regain mobility. In most instances, a little stretching, rolling or hula-hooping the hips will ease the pain and bring normal mobility back again; if not, you should seek medical advice.

> *'I found that the sound of the human voice gained its fullest expression exactly at the point where the singing person – having found the right balance of concentration and tension – could express it bodily.'*
> Alfred Wolfsohn, *Die menschliche Stimme* [*The Human Voice*], 1953

Stand up and sing – but lie down first . . .

The following exercises, to practise lying down, will help you to link movement, breath and voice.

Spinal Stretch (At least 5 minutes)

- Lie down flat on your back.

- Place your two hands, palms downwards, underneath the hollow of your back.

- Stretch out your legs, pushing your heels away from you, flexing the upper part of the foot towards you.

- Remove your hands. Slide your arms up along the floor and stretch them out behind your head.

- Now breathe out and flatten the whole of your back, including the hollow, against the floor. Hold this position for one minute.

- Breathe in and out three or four times. Release.

- Be careful not to flatten your back by pressing downwards from the abdominal muscles, which will constrict your breathing. Flatten your back by visualising inwards to the spine and by moving the lumbar region (the hollow, not the abdominal muscles). Repeat two or three times, as many times a week as you like.

Humming up and down the back (10 minutes)

- In a lying-down position, flat on your back on any hard, supportive surface, bend your knees and place your feet flat on the ground, parallel and apart. Spread out your arms at right angles to your body. Look towards your knees to keep your neck long. Yawn. Sigh.

- Imagine that you have inside you an 'inner keyboard', the keys of which roughly correspond with each of your spinal vertebrae. The higher notes are towards your neck and head, the lower notes are towards your pelvis and tail.

- Take up an easy humming sound and gently hum from the top of your 'keyboard' to the bottom, from low to high and back again.

- Do this a few times, up and down until you get a feeling of high and low in relation to your back and your humming sound.

- If you meet any vocal 'cracks' on the way, don't worry – 'play' around them, include them rather than avoid them, continue sliding the sound where you can. Are you letting the sound move from up to down, from your head to your body *along* your back?

Making a connection between breath and vertebrae (5 minutes)

- Still lying down on your back with your knees bent and feet flat on the ground:

- Keep the cervical spine (back of the neck) long by looking at your knees as you exercise.

- Now, on the next slow out-breath, without humming, lift your pelvis right off the ground by pressing your feet into the ground to give you leverage, and hold it suspended for a moment.

- Breathe in normally through your mouth or nose. On the next slow out-breath, lower your pelvis slowly and gently back to the ground, unrolling your back, vertebra by vertebra, as you do so. Relax. Repeat while humming lightly on the out-breath on the upwards or downwards movement.

Stretching and voicing

Repeat the above 'floor' exercises, voicing E–I–E–I–O! with your mouth open, as you lift and lower your pelvis. While your pelvis is suspended, breathe in.

The object of the exercise is:

- To accompany the movement of your spine with your voice.

- To slide your voice up and down as you move your back up and down. This will help you later, in choosing when to swoop and when not to swoop!

As you repeat this exercise a few times you will gradually fall into an easy up/down flow of sound that accompanies the movement of your back as you lift and lower it. It should be as though the sound is gently sliding from your head to your back, from your back up to and into your head, and from high to low and low to high.

Remember to take an in-breath each time you lift your pelvis, and again when you lower it to the ground. In between, vocalise lightly and easily, up/down, down/up through your body, along your backbone.

At the same time as you are discovering a voice/body connection, by raising and lowering your lower back in this way you will be strengthening your back and thigh muscles. Because of this, don't overdo this exercise at first: with time you will be able to keep it up easily for five minutes at a time. To end the exercise, curl, stretch and roll.

KEEP THE TENSION OUT OF YOUR BACK

Whenever you have been down on the floor, take your time to get back up to your feet. Don't make your back and shoulders tense by doing a rough and jerky forward sit-up and leap. Roll over on to your side and stand up slowly through the sitting-up position, using your hands against the ground to support the lifting up of your back and head. When you are standing up, stretch, open wide your arms, yawn and shake yourself, then feel – and voice – the new energy and freedom in your body.

SINGING FROM THE FEET UP

'On Olivier's advice Vivien Leigh was studying with his teacher,
Elsie Fogarty, who was working hard to lower her voice, starting by
insisting she throw out all her high heels, as she claimed they caused
Vivien's back to go out of alignment, which cramped her lungs.'
Anne Edwards, *Vivien Leigh: a Biography*, 1979

Olivier's teacher made a useful point by encouraging Vivien Leigh to stop wearing high heels. High heels throw the body, and particularly the spinal column, out of balance, or, as it is sometimes called, 'alignment'. You can feel this happen quite clearly, after the first moments of glamour, in front of either the mirror or admiring eyes, have worn off. Any time spent wearing high heels needs to be compensated for by walking barefoot or in flat shoes to stretch out the tendons of the lower leg, and allow the body to regain its natural balance. In fact, any kind of shoes that restrict or cramp the toes or the feet will necessarily have an effect on breathing and energy levels. If your feet are painfully cramped, your energy will be restricted. It is as simple as that.

Finding your centre

By practising these exercises to explore your centre of gravity, you will achieve an awareness that will help you later on, in those moments when you 'stand up and sing'.

In a standing position, wearing flat shoes or none at all, lean straight forward over your toes as far as you can, 'out of alignment'. Notice how hard the muscles in your back have to work to keep you upright. You may find yourself gripping with your toes to stop yourself from falling forwards. Observe your breathing.

Now lean straight backwards onto your heels, again 'out of alignment'; feel the exertion in the region of the abdominal and neck muscles. This 'drawing backwards' tends to happen when you are still not at ease with an audience, and makes your breathing, already affected by anxiety and stage fright, even more stressful. Notice how your breathing is affected when you lean backwards, out of balance and onto your heels.

Now 'play' between the two positions until you find a position that places your weight neither forward over your toes, nor backwards over your heels. Move your weight from the left to the right foot. Find a position that feels central, where your weight is evenly distributed and where your feet, knees, hips, back, shoulders and neck feel relaxed.

Notice whether this position is different from your everyday one. You may find that your habitual posture has moved away from the 'natural', aligned, one and that to regain it, you need to undo restrictive habits.

Repeat this exercise as often as possible, always with bare feet, so that you can be more aware of the extent that you are gripping with your toes or placing weight on your heels.

You will slowly acquire a sense of where your body-weight is, and be able to 'ground' yourself through your central axis.

It is useful to do this exercise with a partner – you can observe each other in profile, and it is immediately obvious to the observer if your body weight is off-centre. With the help of another person's observations, you may be able to discover the extent to which you habitually carry your weight forwards or backwards, thereby unconsciously putting your muscles into tension to keep your body out of balance.

 **The lazy lizard**

(A minimum of 15 minutes for the first time; later on, 5 or 10 minutes will be enough. Repeat twice a week or more)

The following exercise can be practised either as part of a warm-up or to relax you before rest. It is most enjoyable and effective when practised on a floor with a smooth warm surface, as it involves a degree of sliding and rolling of the limbs, which a carpet might snag or impede. It will:

• Rest and invigorate the spinal muscles

• Reconnect movement and breath

• Increase total body awareness

It was inspired originally by an exercise used by the dancer Isadora Duncan, and I have developed it with students over the years, extending its beneficial effects to the study of breathing and voice. A muscular revitalisation follows, prompting all sorts of free rolling and stretching and getting ready for action, vocal or otherwise.

• Throughout the exercise imagine the head and pelvis as 'objects' which turn from side to side as you move.

- Lie flat on your tummy with your head turned to one side. Spread-eagle your arms and legs. Let your weight sink into the floor.

- Think of a basking lizard, visualising the curve in its back as it lies in the sun, legs spread out, soaking up the heat. Stretch out one leg fully, and then, bending the knee of the other leg, slide it upwards at right angles to your body – slowly and lazily.

- Turn your head slightly towards the leg that is pointing downwards.

- In your head, check the straightened leg so that it is pointing downwards in a straight line with your back.

- Open out the fingers of each hand and spread the palms of your hands flat on the ground. You should now have arrived at the position shown in the illustration.

- Rest in that position, letting your weight sink into the ground.

- Feel your heartbeat and the rhythm of your breathing.

- Roll over on your side and bring your knees as close to your nose as possible, then stretch out your whole body, arching your back. Relax.

- Roll over and repeat with the other side of your body. Feel the rotation in your spine. Roll and stretch freely. Stand up slowly, keeping your head down, unrolling your back slowly. Stretch. Yawn. Vocalise.

- Repeat the whole sequence as many times as you wish, resting when you want to.

'A lizard ran out on a rock and looked up, listening
no doubt to the sounding of the spheres.
And what a dandy fellow! The right toss of a chin for you
and swirl of a tail!
If men were as much men as lizards are lizards
they'd be worth looking at.'

D.H. Lawrence, 'Lizard', 1929

Once you get into this exercise you will notice that your 'lazy lizard' can become extremely active: you can then keep up a *continuous movement* from side to side, as long as you make the absolute minimum effort in *sliding* your limbs from one position to the other and by initiating the movement within the backbone.

Singing in the shower

When you next sing in the shower – and who doesn't? – treat it as a free vocal improvisation based on what you have just been learning about the connection between your breath, your voice and your backbone. Practise the vocal 'sing/slide' on the vowel sounds E-I-E-I-O. Use the shower spray to massage and relax your neck as you sing. Improvise vocally, sliding from high to low and low to high, grumbling or growling lazily over, through and around any cracks, stretching out the back of your neck as much as possible. Let your voice swoop, slide and soar without worry or judgement. The humidity is good for your air passages. Splash around in the water and in your voice like a dolphin or whale. Enjoy. Family and friends will eventually get used to it!

PVE, Laughter and the Jaw

'She could never understand how well-bred persons consented
to sing and open their mouths in the ridiculous manner requisite
for that vocal exercise.'
George Eliot, *Middlemarch*, 1871-2

This description of a 'well-bred' attitude towards the wide-open mouth was written almost two centuries ago, but the taboo is still prevalent. The muscles that can exert the most effective restriction on our breathing are the ones we often think about least – those surrounding the upper and lower jaw. Old habits die hard, especially ones taught to us when we are young and impressionable – 'close your mouth!'

Have you ever watched a cat yawn? Or a horse, when it gets a tickle in its nose? They both stretch the jaw wide open. Stretching open the whole jaw to yawn or laugh is one of the pleasures of life! Have you watched a small child laugh? When we are small, laughter seizes us in the middle, throws back our heads, releases our jaws and fills us with exuberant and wonderful energy and breath. Mirth, once touched, bubbles, spills over, erupts, bursts out, explodes, holds its sides, chortles, gasps for breath, streams tears, creases over, rolls about, shrieks and gurgles. At least, it did when we were younger. . .

Laughter is a socially acceptable expression of Primitive Vocal Energy (PVE), which reminds us of our membership of both the human and the animal world and reconnects us with our own body energy, often bringing about a relaxation of the jaw muscles. In early foetal life, the jaw is often compared with the gills of a fish, and in humans it is still directly related to breathing. A dog cannot bark a joyful greeting without fully opening its mouth, and neither can we laugh if we are clamping our jaws together. The sound of your laughter, and your ability to enjoy it, is a very good indication of your potential singing voice – as is your ability to relax and open the lower jaw. Listen to yourself the next time you burst into laughter. Do you hold your hand over your mouth? Do you get short of breath? Is your laughter timid, fruity, sexy, husky, full-throated?

Doctor and opera director Jonathan Miller calls laughter a 'rather peculiar barking convulsion of the respiratory system' (Maria M. Delgado and Paul Heritage, *In Contact with the Gods? Directors Talk Theatre*, 1996).

In laughter, the body sometimes seems to convulse or shake itself to release or even increase powerful emotions. In this way, laughter can have a very beneficial effect on the muscles of breathing and body tone in general. Laughter decreases tension – it causes you to completely empty your lungs, provoking a deep in-breath. It exercises the diaphragmatic muscles and opens the back of the throat (particularly that small sensitive area just above the vocal cords – more in the section The Magic Cords); it releases sound and creates positive energy, and is good for you and for your voice.

Laughter can lead the way to exploring and listening to the resonance in your voice and it can make you more aware of the connection between your body, your voice and your breath.

' 'T' goes through the whole range of her voice on a laugh – I heard her on the telephone the other day,' said 'M'. 'She shrieked up to the top of the scale, then she did a little spin in the middle range – very plummy – and then she went plunging right down into a baritone belly laugh. It was great. And she says she doesn't sing. Just keep on laughing, I say.'

Laughter stimulates the diaphragm: 'I laughed until my sides ached,' we say. This 'ache', which we usually experience as agreeable, rather than disagreeable, comes from the contractions and convulsions of the diaphragm. In turn, this huge muscular convulsion communicates with the rest of the body. If we are able to 'unlock' the jaw as well, our breathing will be deepened, bringing with it a feeling of well-being. If the jaw muscles are tight, we will not be able to experience the pleasure or feeling of release that we seek.

MORE OF A HINDRANCE THAN A HELP

The opera singer Elisabeth Schwarzkopf reportedly said: 'The jaw is not really necessary for singing' (*Masterclass with Elisabeth Schwarzkopf*, KTEH video). The jaw can, in fact, be a positive hindrance; certainly more of a hindrance than a help, much of the time, to singing.

Accustomed to functioning as a nutcracker of no little force, the temporo-mandibular joint of the jaw is capable of exerting upwards of six thousand pounds of pressure per square millimetre. A friend of mine, a hospital nurse, said to me: 'Some people only ever drop their jaw when they die.' A macabre but possibly realistic assessment, considering how tightly most people keep their jaw buckled. Think about how often you consciously or unconsciously clench the jaw and how often you consciously relax it.

A clenched or relaxed jaw? (2 minutes)

- Speak aloud the following phrase through clenched teeth and notice what happens to your breath, and to the sound of your voice:

  A kiss on the hand may be quite continental, but diamonds are a girl's best friend.

- Now relax the jaw – let it *really* drop, and re-read the same phrase:

  Aa kiss on the h-a-an-d may be qui-A—te contin-enta-A-l, bu-t (relax your jaw, breathe in) *di-A-monds Aa-re a girl's be—st frie-nd.*

Didn't the diamonds get bigger? In the first reading, the sound is all squashed up behind the nose; in the second, your out-breath circulates freely, and the sound of your voice fills out warmly. In fact, your voice may even have deepened. Try the same exercise, first clenching and then relaxing the jaw, with the sentence from the Fats Waller song: 'I can't give you anything but love, baby.' Decide which version will convince your lover better.

To enable you to breathe more deeply and to sing your sound out with more freedom, it is the jaw, not the mouth, that needs to 'open wider'. All too often, the instruction to 'open your mouth wider' to sing leads to a sort of uncomfortable grimace. You are forced into an unreal smile; the lips and then your facial and neck muscles are stretched and tense.

Open-jaw check

Trace a line along each of your cheekbones with the fingers of your hands, from nose to ear. Run your fingers along to just in front of your ears, just below the hairline, or in your side-burns if you have them. Move your fingers until you contact a small indentation, just where the joint of the jaw opens. This will be easier if you open and close your jaw a few times.

Tongue and jaw together

Make a NAH-NAH or a NYAH-NYAH sound. This brings your tongue forward up to the hard palate and the tip of it down against your lower teeth. As you say NAH, or NYAH both your tongue and jaw move together into the open position. NAH brings your tongue forward. NYAH helps to flatten it. The tongue contains 19 separate muscles: this is a good moment to relax them. By opening your jaw and bringing the tongue forward, you open up the back of your throat. Practise this until you feel your jaw opening easily and your tongue relaxing in the bottom of your mouth, the front of it against your lower teeth. By the way, this may once again cause a lot of yawning. Enjoy it.

 **Massage**

Push the tips of your forefingers gently against the small indentations in front of the ears, thus 'fixing' the jaw in the open position. Should you experience any stiffness, simply wait before repeating the exercise, and then make sure not to force the movement. Use your fingers to massage all around your ears: in this way, you will help the blood circulation to the complex web of outer muscles connecting the lower jaw to your skull. Sigh. Yawn. Big yawn! Feel the connection between your open jaw and your lower abdomen. Did you feel something relax, which stimulated your yawn? Repeat, keeping your forefingers on the indentation in front of your ears.

This simple exploration will make you more aware of inner connections:

Open jaw – expanded rib cage – diaphragm given optimum space to function – deeper breath.

Repeat as often as you like. The mobility of the jaw is an essential part of the deep in-breath.

A Body Made for Breathing

 **A fast way to a deep in-breath**

Sniff. That's all, just sniff. As though you want to pick up some favourite cooking smell coming from the kitchen. Notice what happens in your body when you sniff. Put your hands on your abdomen, just below the waist. Sniff again. You will notice one of two things: either your chest rises, or your abdomen slightly bulges. For the moment, concentrate on the second version – the slight tummy bulge as you sniff, almost as though you had just swallowed an invisible muffin whole. Notice that the 'muffin' disappears as you breathe out. Try it. For this to be of use to you in singing, you now have to learn to 'sniff' through your mouth. This could be like an expectant gasp. Open your mouth with an expression of surprise. Probably the very act of surprise pulled in that 'sniffed' breath. Practise and feel the 'sniff' in-breath through the nose, and then find a way to achieve the same 'muffin' movement in the abdominal region on the 'expectant' open-mouthed in-breath. It is easy enough to do, and gives you all the air you need to speak or sing quite a long phrase. Try it.

Singing is all about a magical relationship
with the air we breathe.

How easy and free our breathing was when we first arrived in the world, when our simple life was accompanied by the rise and fall of another's breath, and when all we had to do was breathe, listen, look, feel, sleep, eat and grow. So what happens between that blissful time and now, when more often than not the shortest songs and even the simple act of laughing reveals to us all sorts of breathing problems we never even knew we had?

Whatever breathing problems you have now, even if you are unlucky enough to have asthma, you will find that the following exploration and practice will help you overcome many of your limitations.

We must learn to create more space for our in-breath, and develop muscles to enable us to prolong, sustain and play with the out-breath. This is sometimes called 'breath control'.

To sing is to join with and become 'dance partners'
with the air around, breathing it in and then sending it out
full of sound, vibration and meaning.

'Control' is too military a word for this activity, and leads to all sorts of trouble, fear, tension, anxiety and over-work. 'Control your breath!' Often the problem is that we already do control our breathing, but unconsciously. We control it through the ideas we have assimilated about how we 'should' breathe. We think we 'should' breathe from the 'bottom' or the 'top'; we think we 'should' breathe with our mouths closed (very difficult once you start singing!); we think we 'should' have more air, and so on. All these 'shoulds' create inner tension that prevents us from adapting our breathing to whatever physical activity we are engaged in – including singing. When we seek qualities of sound that are different from those we habitually make, we first have to undo habits in the muscular behaviour of our bodies, so we can place and direct our breath differently. All of these habits were developed in response to various circumstances, some of which were unfavourable. In more favourable and unstressed circumstances we can work on undoing or changing old habits. Gradually our breathing will expand. To get to this point often takes time and patience, however quickly we would like to go.

Explore

Learning 'how it works';
MMO (Muscles, Mobility and Openness)
(Periods of 5 to 10 minutes from time to time over the next few days or months)

For this first exploration of your breathing, you will need to find a quiet place to sit, or, even better, somewhere you can lie down or recline comfortably on a flat surface. You can follow much of the exploration, however, from a comfortable armchair while you are reading.

If you are lying down, use a cushion or rolled-up blanket to raise your head a little.

- Loosen any tight clothing, especially belts.

- Rest one hand on your chest and the other on your abdomen. Breathe in and out through your nose with your lips lightly together.

- Observe. Which part of your body moves as you breathe? Is your chest moving? Is your abdomen moving? Together with the relaxation of lying down this may bring on a spate of yawning. Use the yawns; they increase your in-breath – enjoy them, and observe how yawning makes your jaw open and your ribs expand. Yawning is always an excellent preparation for vocalising.

NEXT:

Make each movement clearer to yourself by *exaggerating it* on your in-breath.

- Expand your chest. Expand it even more – on the in-breath. Exaggerate.

- Or push up your abdomen. Push it up even more – on the in-breath. Exaggerate.

- Now reverse the movement. In other words, if you were expanding your chest, now make an abdominal movement, and vice-versa. Feel the difference.

- If you normally lift your chest or rib cage on the in-breath, you may find it difficult to breathe in from the abdomen.

- Conversely, if you have been taught that abdominal breathing is the 'right' way, you may find it strange to lift up the ribs. You may feel an inner obstruction coming from one of those 'shoulds' . . . Should I be doing this? Give it a try. See what happens. You will find that both ways are possible, and that you can 'move' your breath from one part of your body to the other. You can expand either your rib cage or your abdomen on the in-breath.

NEXT:

- Breathe out and wait for the next in-breath. You need not worry that you will expire. No one ever has in this exercise! The call for oxygen comes not from our conscious will but from a chemical signal released by the red blood corpuscles. That in turn triggers the whole process of breathing in. When you can wait no longer, enjoy the in-breath. There is no competition for who can wait the longest! Open up both your abdomen and chest (rib cage) and enjoy the feeling of filling your whole body with air. Do this a number of times.

- Breathe out. Wait. Enjoy the in-breath throughout the whole body. Observe the movements that occur on your in-breath.

NEXT:

- Have you been aware of the feeling of air being 'sucked' in or 'drawn' in? Observe this happening. All you had to do was wait. The vacuum created within your body was enough, together with the signal for oxygen.

NEXT:

- In a sitting up or standing position, breathe in and then blow out on an out-breath as actively as possible, like a deflating balloon – 'whoosh', through the lips. Without pausing, let your body pull in the next breath through the nose. Do this two or three times. Did you lift your shoulders? Next time try *not* to lift your shoulders, just allow the rib cage to expand as you breathe in.

NEXT:

- Repeat, but put the emphasis of movement lower down, in the abdominal region. Think of blowing out the air 'whoosh' on a prolonged fffffffffffffffff sound, and then let your abdomen expand with a fast in-breath. Feel the air being sucked into the vacuum you have created in your body in a different way from when you expanded your rib cage – more like the 'sniff' in-breath. Try one way and then the other. Alternate. If you have one, practise this with a silk handkerchief, or a piece of very light silk chiffon, held in front of your mouth.

Discover

You have discovered two distinct movements related to the normal in-breath: an expansion in the chest region (i.e. the rib cage), and a movement in the abdominal area. You are able to use two different structures. How clearly can you make yourself a clear physical picture of what is going on 'in there' and 'down there'? What makes the top of your body expand? What makes your abdomen expand?

Explore

The rib cage and breastbone (10 minutes)

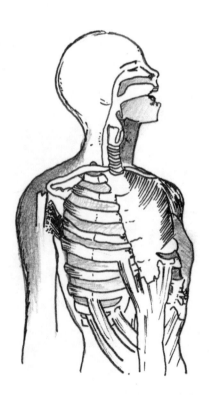

• Sitting or lying down, explore with your fingertips the base of the rib cage. This would definitely give you the giggles if anyone else did it, but is fine for you. As children we often 'hooked' our fingers up inside the base of our ribs – you may be able to do this. Trace a path right around your body, at the base of your ribs. Roll over on to your side, first one side and then the other, and try to tuck your fingers up inside the lower ribs. Are you surprised to find how low down they are? How close to the hip-bones? Make yourself a mental image of the shape of your own rib cage.

• Locate the breastbone, the hard structure known as the sternum that runs down the middle of your chest, from the base of your neck to the base of the ribs. Trace a line from the base of your breastbone right round to your backbone. That's a big structure.

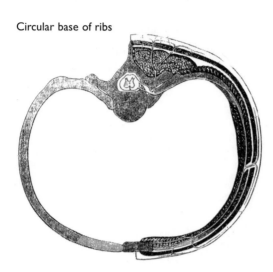

Circular base of ribs

• Now try and 'take hold' of the base of your ribs in front and then give a little cough. Did you feel as though something inside was pushing your fingers away? Try it again, holding on as firmly as possible to the base of your ribs. Give a little cough.

• Now, holding on in the same way, on the *in-breath* 'blow up' the abdominal area, making a fat tummy. Did you feel your ribs 'slipping' away from your fingers again? Repeat.

• Now contract your abdominal muscles. In the lying-down position this is easily done by just lifting your head up and looking at your feet, or lifting your legs together up to an angle of forty-five degrees. Try and 'blow up' your abdomen on the *in-breath* at the same time. Repeat, observing what happens and what it feels like. Did you feel pressure in your throat? Breathe in again without contracting your abdominal muscles. Did your throat feel looser?

CLEARING UP A CONFUSION

I would like you to try and feel the difference between two sets of muscles, and to clear up some confusion about 'abdominal breathing'. Hopefully you will have become aware of muscles other than your abdominal ones in the previous exercise.

Discover

The body's best-kept secret

While holding onto the base of your ribs with your fingers, you may have felt the strength of a muscle that seemed to pull the ribs inwards and away from you as you coughed; that hidden strength came from the diaphragm.

The diaphragm is one of the best-kept secrets in the body. It is much more than just a wavy black line through your middle, as so often portrayed in diagrams. Well hidden, impossible to see and difficult to feel, it is the largest single muscle in the body. It is the major muscle of respiration, without which, as we shall see, the lungs would not be of much use to us.

Even though we cannot feel the diaphragm directly, we can learn to directly influence its movements.

By learning about the behaviour of the diaphragm, you will see how this extra 'inside' knowledge can add to the feeling of 'grounding' your voice, and give support to your singing.

- Trace a line, with the fingers of one hand, down your breastbone (sternum) again until you reach its base, where you feel a little hollow.

- Push your two forefingers firmly into this hollow; again, give a little cough.

- Observe how 'something' moves and jerks your fingers outwards.

- Do it again, pushing your forefingers in even more firmly, without discomfort. Give another little cough.

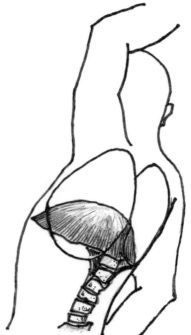

Your diaphragm makes a massive contraction at your command, as you cough to eject air rapidly. A normal cough ejects air at 600 miles per hour (mph). This is probably the equivalent of a dog's bark.

To test the strength of your diaphragm, you could think about making a few energetic and welcoming yapping sounds…You will feel the diaphragm literally bouncing inside! (When you sneeze, air is expelled at a rate of 103mph as a result of the upward and inward contraction of the diaphragm.)

The diaphragm in relation to the spine and lungs.

THINK BIG

The diaphragm is a large circular muscle, attached to the entire perimeter of the base of the ribs, higher in the front than in the back. If you have difficulty in imagining the full circumference of the diaphragm, think of the waistline of a fully pregnant woman. Even if you are slim-waisted, the circumference of your diaphragm is still large – unless you are wearing a corset, of course.

A FLOOR AND A CEILING

The diaphragm divides the body, separating it in two. It creates a 'floor' for the lungs and the heart to rest upon, and a 'ceiling' for all the organs of digestion, excretion and reproduction below it. Whenever it moves, everything above and below is affected. If it moves very little, nothing much moves; if it moves a lot, everything moves a lot. As well as being the major muscle of respiration, it is in some ways the inner body's secret masseur.

The diaphragm is roughly the shape and size of a large swimming hat: large enough for you to put the top of your head (if you could) underneath it. Get a friend to rest their head on your abdomen to help you visualise and feel the dimensions of this huge muscle. Give a little cough while their head is resting there, and notice the strength of the muscle!

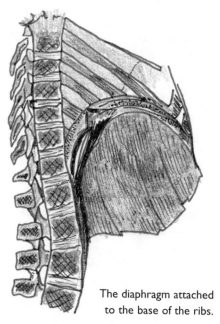

The diaphragm has two main movements that are important for us to know about.

- Contraction upwards and inwards towards its centre (the phrenic centre, fed by the phrenic nerve) on the out-breath.

- Contraction downwards and outwards to the base of the ribs on the in-breath.

The diaphragm attached to the base of the ribs.

These two movements are worth giving some thought to. They do not feel obvious, but understanding them will make a lot of difference to your ability to find 'support' for your breathing. A large part of diaphragm action, happily, is beyond our conscious control. Much of its work is a lower brain function, triggered by signals from the phrenic nerve set off by oxygen levels in the red blood cells, but an important part of its functioning happens only as a result of our conscious will.

DROP THAT WEIGHT

Realising the comparative weight of the diaphragm might help you to be able to let go of it and let it drop down on the in-breath. The diaphragm drops on the in-breath as much by its own weight as by the peripheral contraction and outward/upward pull of the lower ribs. Sniff inwards: feel it drop!

- We can and do, consciously or unconsciously, increase or decrease the amount of air we breathe in.

- We can influence the speed and pressure with which the out-breath leaves our body through muscular movements of rib cage and diaphragm.

MORE CONFUSIONS

One of my students was confused at this point.

'Doesn't the air fill the lungs on its own,' she asked. 'I mean, do we have to do anything at all for the air to get into the lungs?'

'How does it get in, then?' I asked.

'Well . . . ' she hesitated. 'It comes in through here,' she said, indicating her nose and mouth.

'How? Does it push its way in?'

'No . . . not exactly.'

'Let's imagine for a moment that it does, what would that feel like?'

'Like on a very windy day,' said another student. 'It's horrible, you feel the air being forced into your mouth, and then you can't breathe at all!'

CONSCIOUS CONTROLS
AND INFLUENCES UPON THE DIAPHRAGM

- When we breathe out, a vacuum is created in the lungs as a result of the upward/inward contraction of the diaphragm.

- To breathe in again, the diaphragm relaxes its centre and contracts around its perimeter, thus enlarging the inter-costal space (the space between the ribs) and drawing air into the lungs.

This is where our conscious thought can influence and extend the natural movement.

The periphery of the diaphragm is attached to the base of the ribs, right? All round. If we expand our ribs we are also pulling the diaphragm out with the ribs. Try it. Expand your ribs. Hold your breath. Think. Where is the diaphragm now, and what is it doing? By holding your breath and expanding your ribs, you are effectively preventing the diaphragm from its usual upwards/inwards contraction. You are slowing down its action through contractions of the inter-costal muscles. Relax.

We can't hold onto the diaphragm with our hands as we can the swimming hat, but we can learn to restrain its natural return through 'widening' and lifting the lower ribs.

THE POWER OF THE DIAPHRAGM

'But,' said my student, 'what about abdominal breathing? When I blow up my tummy on an in-breath, isn't air going into it? I mean, what else makes it expand? I've been taught to breathe into the abdomen; I thought the air went down there – everybody said it did.'

Remember, the diaphragm effectively divides the body in half; the heart and lungs and all the air passages lie *above* the diaphragm, and the organs to do with digestion and reproduction lie *below* the diaphragm. It is a floor to the lungs and a ceiling to the abdomen. The only way for air to leave the lungs is through the nose and/or mouth.

In 'blowing-up' your abdominal region, you are not conducting air into that area – your descending diaphragm is actually pushing the abdominal contents, i.e. all the soft structures, downwards. This is what creates that extra bulge below the waistline. At the same time, you are making more space above the waistline for the lungs to expand and draw in more air. When you expand the rib cage in the same way, you are creating more space for the lungs.

THE LAZY LUNGS

Think of your lungs as basically lazy, lazier even than the lizard just 'hanging' there: they are literally liable to shrink unless pulled. The lungs, made of spongy, non-muscular tissue, are dependent on structures related to them for movement. The outer surface of each lung adheres to the inner surfaces of the rib cage and the upper surface of the diaphragm by means of a special lining called the pleura.

- When the diaphragm moves, the lungs move with it.
- When the ribs expand, the lungs expand with them.

It is the regular expansion/contraction of the diaphragm, stimulated by blood oxygen levels, that is principally responsible for all lung movement. To this influence can be added, in normal healthy mobile bodies, a small but all-over expansion of the rib cage.

But, equally, the rib cage can lose mobility and become little more than a case for the lungs, simply contracting inwards when we breathe out, because it is being pulled inwards by the action of the diaphragm. The lungs are made of an elastic tissue that, in a healthy body, can stretch quite dramatically in all directions when pulled – but which will never stretch on its own.

We have to train ourselves to resist the natural inward/upward pull of the diaphragm when we want to sustain an out-breath.

To prolong or sustain an out-breath you must enter the *muscular play* between diaphragm and ribs. Learning how to co-ordinate these two complementary body structures is fundamental to breath support and 'control', and to your enjoyment of singing. The whole process is relatively easy and quick to learn because you are following and expanding the natural movements of your body.

More support for your voice from hidden muscles, above and below the belt

'Get to the bottom of the garden if you're going to make that noise!'

'Belting' is the name given to a certain kind of sound that has been part of the range of the human voice since we first yelled at each other across the primeval mud flats.

Finding the 'belting' qualities in the voice is more to do with undoing mental attitudes that inhibit expressions of high vocal energy in the first place than with learning a new and difficult vocal task. The power to 'belt' out the voice comes as much from being mentally and physically motivated towards making the sound (the feeling/intention: why am I doing it, and what is it about?) as it does from finding the ability to support and sustain the breath.

Two sets of muscles to add support to your voice

The purpose of support is as much to take pressure off the throat and vocal folds as to *sustain* the outflow of breath. To do this more effectively, you now need to find the muscles round your waist from front to back (the transverse muscles). You feel them when you cough or sneeze. These muscles can be trained to play a more useful role in breath support than the famous 'sit-up' muscles, the abdominus rectus.

Opposite: keys to finding your voice's hidden power.

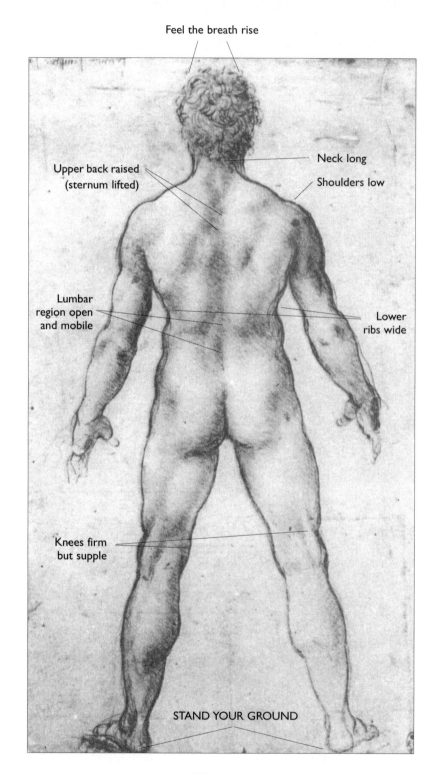

Feel the breath rise

Neck long

Shoulders low

Upper back raised
(sternum lifted)

Lumbar
region open
and mobile

Lower
ribs wide

Knees firm
but supple

STAND YOUR GROUND

- Turn your inner focus to your waist (whether large, small or non-existent!)

- Try, instead of pulling in your tummy, to draw in your waist all the way round – a small but clear movement. Did you feel that?

- Now repeat on the in-breath, at the same time expanding your rib cage.

- Keeping the rib cage expanded, breathe out.

- Breathe in again and *relax* the tummy muscles.

- It should feel as though you are lifting the rib cage up from underneath.

- Be careful not to lift your shoulders. Try it a few times.

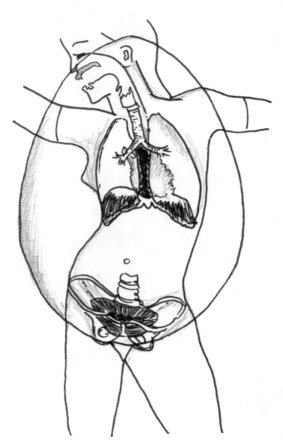

The egg-shape can help you to include both what is above and what is below in your visualisations of the body.

Notice how this egg-shape keeps an area in focus from the open space at the back of the nose right down to the pelvic floor.

THE MUSCLES OF THE PELVIC FLOOR
AS A SUPPORT TO BREATHING

Women, especially those who have gone through childbirth, are familiar with the pelvic floor – sometimes described as a 'lower diaphragm'. To a greater or lesser degree, it works in tandem with the diaphragm. It is this area between the pelvis and the diaphragm that is referred to as the plexus, or as the 'hara' in yoga. The 'hara' is the seat of energy and power. The pelvic floor is a muscular structure, rather like a hammock, slung inside the pelvic bones and the surrounding anal, urethral and vaginal openings, just as it holds or contains all the sexual and digestive organs above it.

Try and create a mental picture of the 'dome' of the diaphragm and the 'basin' or 'hammock' of the pelvic floor. This area is also known as the seat of the emotions. The ability to contract, expand and relax muscular structures within it helps to keep everything – and not just the emotions – flowing healthily!

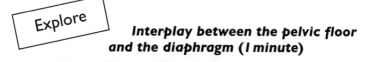

Interplay between the pelvic floor and the diaphragm (I minute)

- In a sitting position, place a hand underneath your bottom, then cough lightly or make a little yapping sound. You should feel pressure on your hand as the perineum, or pelvic floor, is pushed downwards by increased intra-abdominal pressure.

- Now try and keep the ribs expanded outwards as you cough again. The pressure is different: now it is divided between the diaphragm and the pelvic floor. Interplay between the diaphragm and the pelvic floor gives your breath greater support and will help to give you a feeling of greater control, especially when singing long phrases or holding strong feelings or sustained volume.

Classical singing teachers sometimes ask pupils to train their pelvic floor muscles by 'holding' a coin between the buttocks while singing. Squeezing your buttocks may help you to locate the actual deep muscles *inside* the pelvis, and eventually you will be able to contract them without resorting to coins!

BREATHING RESTRICTIONS

'A foggy day in London town,
Had me low, and it had me down,
I viewed the morning with much alarm,
The British Museum had lost its charm.'

Ira Gershwin, 'A Foggy Day',
from *A Damsel in Distress*, 1937

As we all know only too well, how we feel has an immediate effect on our breathing. Despondency, alarm, elation or depression all influence our breathing. These emotions can build up patterns of muscular activity that can either free or restrict the movement of the rib cage and diaphragm. Tight shoulder muscles, painful neck muscles or rigid inter-costal muscles can all restrict the full deep breath we need to give our singing vitality. When understanding better how the anatomy works, you can, in moments of emotion or stress, remember the muscular structures and reverse unconscious processes by working towards relaxing, opening, expanding and steadying your breathing. You can, through muscular effort, influence and re-educate your patterns of breathing. This will eventually be very helpful to you in moments of performance anxiety, whether onstage or off.

Experiment with soft breath and sound.
When the sound rings clear, however strong, the candle flame will not move.

An active life

Swimming, rowing, dancing of all kinds, especially African, South American, flamenco, salsa and Oriental; these are the kinds of activities which, with anatomical awareness, will help you ground your body and develop good open breathing habits. Take long walks in the countryside or through city parks, swinging your arms and expanding your rib cage. Investigate Alexander Technique, Feldenkreis Movement Awareness, stretching classes, T'ai Chi, Chi Gong or yoga. All these movement disciplines help you to centre your body energies. More active physical sports will help you develop stamina, which is another quality essential for your body/breath/voice relationship. Try to develop movements such as rolling, reaching, turning, bending and twisting wherever you can in everyday life, even if this only means changing the way you get out of bed in the mornings! Open your jaw wide, yawn your rib cage into open expansion and greet the new day.

More singing in the shower

Repeat the 'fun' exercise as described on page 57. This time, be aware of your expanded rib cage, lengthened neck and open jaw. Sing/slide your voice up and down, feeling it move from high to low in relation to your long, snake-like backbone. Enjoy your sound. Let your voice dance lightly from one sound to another. Improvise from high to low and from low to high, 'sgrumbling' gently around any vocal cracks, invent your own melodies. Use the force of the shower to massage and invigorate your whole body, and especially to relax your neck. Include a few NAH or NYAH sounds, if no one is around, to remind yourself to bring your tongue forward and open the back of your throat. And remember – when you make more space for your lungs, you are also making more space for your heart.

Imagination, breathing, inner listening

> 'By the fine, fine wind that takes its course
> through the chaos of the world ...'

D.H. Lawrence, 'Song of a Man who has Come Through', 1917

At a quiet time of day, take a few minutes to imagine yourself sitting on a wide empty beach somewhere, watching the sea, listening to the waves. The pounding crash of each new wave swishes along the shore, singing overtones into infinity. You strain to follow the symphony of its rippling race ... And the next wave rises, curls, breaks – and again, it lifts ... draws back ... curls ... breaks ... like a gigantic breathing.

Now with your eyes closed, in a quiet moment, try to feel this same deep, calm, rhythmic movement in your own breathing.

'I'd really like to be looking up at the stars and listening to the sea.'
Robbie Williams, British pop singer

The Magic Cords:
where Breath turns into Sound

The miraculous vibration of vocal sound is set in motion by a signal from the brain, together with the passage of the out-breath through a very small structure suspended inside the throat: the larynx. The larynx is in a highly strategic position in the body. It is hanging suspended towards the front of the neck, exactly at the bridge point between head and body. A sound vibrator of amazing versatility, it nestles against a complex muscular mesh of vital passageways, some of which transport blood to and from the brain and some of which carry food to the stomach. In action, it vibrates close to the cervical spine that protects the major nerve pathways flowing to and from the cerebral cortex. The larynx is wrapped around by the thyroid, the hormonal gland responsible for

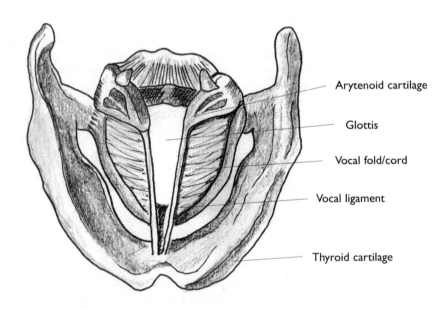

Arytenoid cartilage

Glottis

Vocal fold/cord

Vocal ligament

Thyroid cartilage

The larynx, viewed from above.

metabolic levels, and is close to another gland, the thymus, whose real function is still largely undiscovered. The larynx is comparatively close to the eyes, the ears, the brain and the heart.

The larynx has two major functions: to keep the airways clear of mucus, fluid or food, and to create sound. Remember, for survival reasons we are born noisy creatures – we are programmed to respond vocally. As we go through the socialising process, we learn to contain our vocal reactions to internal and external stimuli, but our breathing rhythms are constantly influenced by the impressions we perceive through our five senses, whether or not we give voice. Every breath we take, of every kind, goes in and out through the magic cords within the larynx.

MEETING THE BOARD OF CENSORS

Imagine that everything you have ever felt: happiness, sorrow, love or jealousy; every pounding of the heart or ache in the loins; every rage let out, or anger swallowed; every joy shared in song, were all registered by the tissues and muscles of the body. Imagine that your every emotion is met and censored in the throat by the watcher in the brain: this feeling we can give voice to, respond to, that one must be suppressed into silence. Every single emotion we feel moves through that same small organ of sound that embraces our inward and outward breath. It is not surprising that we sometimes feel a tightening in the throat.

The larynx

- Put the thumb and forefinger of one hand lightly upon the front of your throat and rest them there for a moment as you read. Move your fingers a little below your chin, to find the bump of your 'Adam's apple' (both men and women have one) and make a swallowing movement. You will feel a hard bony structure rise and fall as you swallow – the swallowing movement that occurs in the digestive tract (the pharynx) above and behind it causes the larynx to move. Therefore you can immediately confirm that *the larynx is a mobile structure.* This may seem a small point to make, but knowing it will give you a greater sense of freedom when you sing – instead of worrying about the movement, you can try varying it, and discover what happens to the sound of your voice when the larynx moves.

- Put your forefingers lightly on your Adam's apple once again, and move your fingers very lightly until you find a small bony protrusion at the centre – it feels almost as though you were touching a chicken's 'wishbone'. Some vocalists have found a similarity with a ship's prow – a very small magic prow. Keep your forefinger lightly on the skin over this spot.

- Yawn and notice how it goes down.

- Sing/slide your voice into a squeak, and observe how it rises. Make a swallowing movement again and notice how it moves up and down.

The lower the larynx moves, the deeper the tone; the higher up it goes, the higher the tone. Experiment. You could make 'gobbling' sounds like a turkey, and feel it move even more. Classical singers use this mobility when singing 'trills' – alternating between two neighbouring frequencies very fast. Yodellers use the mobility in another way, moving rapidly between a high and low pitch to make that unmistakable sound. Close the door, put on some loud music to fool the neighbours, and try it! YODEL-EH-EE-EH!

A HEALTHY LARYNX IS A MOBILE LARYNX

At its base, the larynx is fixed to the trachea, or windpipe; at the top it is suspended, hanging a bit like a sock on a peg, on a little floating bone (the hyoid) embedded in the muscles of the front of the neck, and opening into the back of the throat. The hyoid is made of both muscle and cartilage, but not bone, and is intended to move.

MAKING SOUND WAVES

In appearance and function, the larynx is somewhat like a highly sophisticated nozzle. You may not have come across this description of the larynx in other books on the voice, and scientists might raise an eyebrow or two, but there is a similarity. Think what a nozzle does; it regulates the outflow of whatever is in the tube or hose connected to it. The larynx is a very finely tuned 'nozzle' that can regulate the speed and pressure of the air coming up from our lungs whenever we vocalise, sing or speak. The larynx, home to the magic cords, will have more freedom of movement the more space we allow it by keeping the whole neck long and mobile.

THE LENGTHENING OF THE NECK

Scientists and musicians alike agree that the lengthening of the neck, or windpipe, and the evolution of the larynx from what was formerly just a short tube, is partially responsible for our unique ability to fine-tune our vocalisations into sophisticated speech or song. Sound waves are modified according to the length of the windpipe they go through. A longer windpipe produces a deeper sound. In his book *The Life of Birds*, David Attenborough observes that 'cranes, which produce trombone-like calls, have windpipes that are so long they curl into loops alongside the keel of their breastbones.' The presence of the magic cords and the length of the neck give us more possibilities than our ape ancestors to regulate the outgoing air speed and pressure, thus allowing us to fine-tune vocal sound. Wind instruments operate on the same principle: the length and diameter of the tube determines the sounds available. In humans, unlike musical instruments, both length and diameter are pliable and modifiable: we can, through small muscular adjustments, shorten or lengthen the 'inner tube' from larynx to mouth and we can increase or decrease different parts of its diameter or openings.

To prepare throat and neck for exploratory exercises

- From a sitting position, begin by 'snaking' your fingers, wrists, elbows, shoulders, shoulder blades and spine, thus releasing tension from the trapezius muscle.

- Repeat the neck lengthening exercise given on page 49 (the 'three keys'). Release your jaw, yawning as you do so.

- Be careful not to pull your chin inwards in military fashion: this will defeat the objective of lengthening the neck without tension.

A secret inner mouth

Within the larynx, and protected by it, are stretched the magic cords which have the unique function of transforming the outgoing air into vibrations or sound waves. The word 'cords' is a bit confusing, leading one to imagine anything from fine thread to skipping rope! In fact, what you find inside the larynx, or 'voice box', are not cords at all but what look rather like two small, moist, pearly grey 'lips', called more accurately vocal *folds*. This little inner mouth, carefully protected within the larynx, stretches across the trachea, a little above the point where it becomes the larynx. It is this curiously lip-like structure that is the real 'fine tuner' of the human voice.

How big are these folds? Approximately 12.5mm to 17mm in a fully-grown woman and between 17mm and 25mm in an adult man. You could visualise the two folds, when closed, as a little pair of 'lips', sitting, not from left to right as the lips of the mouth, but from the front to the back of the throat.

Feeling the folds

Whisper very quietly the word PUP. Now, with the lips barely parted, whisper in quick succession on a gentle out-breath: P P P P PUP. Now P – UP-UP. Now, still with the lips of your mouth parted, whisper just UH-UH-UH – you will feel the sound in your throat – as though you were going to say UP, but just get as far as UH. By now you should feel the sound being formed in your throat, and as long as you are not actually making a voiced sound, you will hear, and feel, the movement and location of your vocal folds. It is a very short, soft 'popping' or 'clicking' sound. Alternate the P-P-P-P sound you make with the lips of your mouth and with the folds on UH-UH-UH.

In saying P-P-P-P, your lips open and close over your mouth, interrupting the out-flow of air. The inner lips, or muscular folds, come together similarly like small wedges to interrupt the out-breath in the throat. They '*adduct*' and come edge to edge, or lip to lip. When they '*abduct*', or open, they allow the breath to pass between them once more in small 'puffs' or waves of sound. (When we are breathing normally they are relaxed and abducted.) In that exploratory exercise you were effectively slowing down the vibration of your vocal folds. You will notice that the volume of sound made was minimal – and the pitch was low.

Making a secret smile

The unique positioning of these 'inner lips' allows us to practise a truly 'secret smile' from back to front, rather than from side to side. Try it. Hum very, very gently as you smile. Put your forefingers on the 'prow' of your larynx and feel the buzz.

GOOD VIBRATIONS

The vocal folds vibrate, and have a fantastic ability to vary the speed of vibration. This is partly due to the uniquely soft and resilient type of muscle of which they are formed. This has the ability to 'undulate' upon itself over each of the two ligaments that actually are 'string-like'. Fortunately, like most of the actions of the folds, we do not have to do anything consciously to enable this wonderful undulation to happen. It occurs whenever we give voice.

FREQUENCY

The frequency of vibration of the folds determines the musical note or pitch of the sound created. The greater the vibration, the higher the pitch or frequency;

the slower the vibration, the lower the pitch, or frequency of the sound. In the following exploration we will explore the *slowest* vibrations and therefore the *lowest* frequency or pitch available to us.

Think frogs! (5 to 10 minutes)

- Moisten your lips and bring them together to make the kind of motor sound young children like to do: BRRRRR-BRRRR. BRRRRRRR! Feel the vibration in your lips. It could get quite ticklish or wet!

- Now with lips slightly apart, start the gentle PUP-UH-UH-UP sound at the level of the vocal folds again on the out-breath, and now as you are doing it think of frogs. Yes, frogs! Begin to croak. On the out-breath. Arrrrrrrrrrrrr. The less you do, the better it works. Relax the jaw. (If you have actual mucus or phlegm 'frogs' in your throat now, refer to the passage below). Imagine yourself now as a large bull-frog with a huge pouch below your chin. Think lazy, low sounds. Relax your tongue, with the tip against the lower teeth.

- Try and let the sound come without forcing: Arrrrrrrrrrrrr. Yawn some more, then repeat from the PUP-UH-UP stage. This is a good exercise to do with a fellow frog for company. Have a dialogue!

Fast and slow frequencies and the larynx

You are setting in motion *and slowing down* the frequency-producing movement of the folds, producing a very low frequency (or pitch) of adduction/abduction, a slow emission of sound waves and therefore a low, almost discontinuous, sound. This sound will, however, stimulate the blood circulation to the vocal muscles and will, hopefully, give you a sense of enjoyment. Relax and repeat on the next out-breath – remember to widen the ribs to resist the diaphragmatic return and prolong your out-breath. Don't worry if you don't achieve the desired sound straight away; when you can make a clear mental sound picture of this peculiarly guttural sound, it will come.

This little exploration/exercise has the potential to teach you something about *finding a balance between effort and relaxation*; you need both to achieve it, as with most vocalising!

You could try repeating this exercise in the shower: the humidity and steam will make it even more enjoyable – and you will feel even more like a frog!

A FROG IN YOUR THROAT

Explorations focusing on the throat are likely to reveal those other well-known 'frogs' that gather there unwanted. These could be anything from an undefined 'lump', a bit of phlegm, or an overflow of saliva or mucus that blurs and covers over the clear sounds we want. It is natural for phlegm to gather in the throat. Mucus membranes in the throat, mouth and nasal passages must be kept moist – we would be very uncomfortable and quite unable to sing if they were dry! The best way to deal with undesirable amounts of phlegm or mucus is:

- Wait for it to go away naturally through the swallowing reflex.

- Gently cough to encourage it up and out of the larynx and into the neighbouring digestive tube. Avoid violent coughing, which puts undue pressure onto the vocal folds. Do you really need to give your throat a 600mph kick?

- Take a drink of water or other liquid, but not milk.

- Yawn and then swallow actively a few times.

- Carry on regardless!

Explore

Turning the frog into a prince
(2 to 3 minutes)

- With your lips slightly apart, start the PUP-UH-UH-UP sound from the inner lips, or folds, on the out-breath. Remember – this should not be a rough or breathy sound, but a soft clear sound, almost like clicking. Then gradually 'think' it into a soft, low, easily sustainable singing sound: AAAAH. You may feel the singing sound *below* the clicking sound. The less you do, the better it works. Feel the vibration.

- Hold a hand up close to your mouth and feel the moist warmth on the air coming out. Relax. Repeat. If you think of yourself as having a small high voice you may be surprised at the depth of the voice in this exercise. Soft and low, not loud. Think the sound even lower, down towards the breastbone, and repeat. Place your hands over the breast-bone to feel the vibration of sound in your chest area. Observe how very little effort is required to set this low sound singing once you have found it.

Choosing to be true or false

Perhaps you have experienced a breathy sound, rather than the clear sound you were seeking. You may have been using what are known as 'the false folds'.

They are two mucous membranes (a body tissue similar to the inside of the mouth) in the larynx just above the true cords. Try to think a little deeper, just below them. *The sound of the 'true' folds coming together edge to edge is a clear 'clicking' sound.* Both kinds of sound can be achieved by the prompting of your imagination. It is useful to know you can choose between false or true folds: breathy or clear sound.

 ***Play between breathy and clear spoken sounds – ready, willing and able***

The 'lips,' or 'folds', are attached together at one end to the inside of the 'prow', or front of the larynx. At their other end, they are *separately attached* to two little pyramid-shaped cartilages (the arytenoids) which have the ability to pivot. This enables them to bring the folds edge to edge during phonation (voicing), or, by pivoting the other way, to keep the airway open during normal respiration. The folds, in connection with the power supply and resonating fields of head and body, are in principle ready, willing and able to give voice through an entire pitch range from high to low and from loud to soft, over a huge variation of texture and wordless expression – all in response to your thought and feeling!

THE GLOTTIS: THE HOLE IN THE MIDDLE

The space or hole between the two folds is called the glottis. The magical and muscular folds can change the shape of the glottis, making it narrower or wider at any place along the length of the two lips. Try to whistle, at any point between the two lips of your mouth. As you will see, whistling from the corner of your mouth is no easy thing! *The folds can 'whistle' almost anywhere along their length in response to our thought.*

The 'glottal stop', used by yodellers and some Tzigane singers, is when the two lips come firmly together to stop the out-going air. You can discover this simply by making an easily sustainable singing sound and then stopping it 'in the throat'. Practise making the sound together with a firm gesture of 'Stop!' 'Ah-Ah!' This will be similar to the sounds made in karate, or other martial arts exercises.

LIKE THE PUPIL IN A CAT'S EYE

Have you ever looked into the pupil of a cat's eye? Take a look when the sun is high, or the light is bright, and that typical black 'slit' in the cat's green or golden eye closes to almost nothing – just a thin black line, or not even that. The iris of cats' eyes (the green or golden part) and of our eyes too, of course, is light-sensitive. The vocal folds are sensitive to our thought, our imagination, our memories, our feelings and to external sound. They change shape, contracting and expanding at the least suggestion or impulse from our brains. Once again, all we have to do is remove any muscular tensions or restrictions around this extraordinary natural mechanism and then just let it go – with the music – in response to the directions of our thought and imagination.

HEARING AND VOICING: THE PHYSICAL LINK

Neither the larynx nor any other part of the body should be investigated independently of their neighbouring structures. The passages that take air into the lungs pass through the nose and mouth, the back of the mouth and the back of the throat – and even the ears. Everything is connected to everything else. Two small tubes connect the inner ear to the back of the throat: they are called the Eustachian tubes. They are responsible for maintaining the correct balance of pressure between the air outside and the air inside the body. The ears convey the physical vibration of sound we hear to the back of the throat and thus to the larynx, establishing a clear physical connection between hearing and voicing. Our ears hear and feel sound. In this way, hearing is more closely connected to skin and the sense of touch than you would imagine. The immediacy with which we humans are able to reproduce and imitate sounds comes in part from this connection, and from our ability to trust our own natural resources. It is like birds trusting the air to carry them. When too much thinking, hesitation, worry and doubt slows down or interferes with the natural speed with which connections can be made between ear and voice, we are likely to sing 'off-key' or 'falsely.'

The feel of sound

Do you remember as a child making buzzing sounds from a comb wrapped in a piece of paper? The following exploration is to underline the difference of quality between a normal out-breath and an out-breath that is turned into sound vibration (voiced).

- Hold a piece of lightweight writing paper close to your mouth with both hands, fingers spread.

- Breathe in and out normally against the paper. What do you experience?

- Now set your out-going breath into sound vibration on an easily sustainable open-mouthed AAA, or HAA sound. Do you feel the paper vibrating against your fingertips?

- Repeat with different vocal qualities from very soft to loud: notice the difference in vibration.

Drums and gongs can give us experience of sound vibration – the well-known percussionist Evelyn Glennie relies on this fact to compensate for her deafness, feeling and thus 'hearing' sound.

MEMORY AND MUSICAL PITCH

The sensory link between the ears and the voice enables us to imitate or reproduce musical sound in quality and pitch. Moreover, the vocal folds will faithfully emit whatever pitch of sound we are able to remember and bring clearly into our minds. Some people have this ability to a remarkable degree – they have what is known as 'pitch memory' or 'perfect pitch', just as some people have a colour memory, or highly accurate verbal memory. How much of this ability is a natural one, reinforced by positive external influences from an early age, is not always known.

EMPATHY AND LISTENING

The little 'internal mouth' is extremely sensitive to every suggestion of the imagination, and even works soundlessly, responding to our thoughts, aware of our impulses to speak or sing. You may have noticed too that the folds respond empathetically to others as we listen to them, and in sympathy with outside sounds and vibrations – we can sometimes feel in our own throats the sound someone else is voicing, or a difficulty they may be experiencing in reaching a certain high or low pitch.

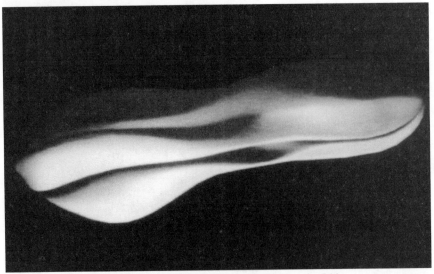

Folds? No, very similar in appearance but not the folds:
the human embryo before the limbs develop.

SOUND STORAGE

And here is another thought: given the opportunity, the folds will allow us to express sounds we didn't even know we had. This suggests perhaps that the body itself contains, within the vocal folds, sound memories.

All the fantastic qualities of the magic cords would come to naught were it not for the body and mind of the person who owns them, and the mobility and openness of the physical structures around the cords: remember, they sit in a passageway. No one as yet has been able to take out the larynx, complete with folds/cords, put it on a table and get it to sing!

To find more enjoyment in your voice, laugh and cry when you want to; rest when you can and need to – pauses are important; have the courage of your convictions; find a way to communicate your thoughts and feelings, and whenever possible, in the shower, the car, with friends, in the practice studio on your own, explore the magic sounds of your voice – cracks and all.

> *'What's so remarkable about being born with a whistle in your throat?'*
> Aristotle Onassis to the singer Maria Callas

Taking the weight of your head off your neck

- Sitting forward on a chair, undo tight clothing around your waist, lean the upper part of your body forwards over your knees, or, if that is uncomfortable, rest your elbows and forearms on your knees. Allow your head to hang.

- Allow your back to expand on the in-breath. Breathe in and out calmly.

- Let your head swing gently on 'yes-yes', 'maybe' and 'no-no' movements.

- When you want to sit up again, unroll your upper body slowly through your back, letting the head hang for as long as possible. Bring your chest forward slightly as you sit up, and allow your head to find the upright position without jerking it upwards suddenly.

- In the upright position, make little 'yes-yes', 'no-no' and 'maybe/perhaps' movements with the head. Feel your neck opening and lengthening.

Do you want to sing? Say YES! Y.E.S.S.S.S.S.S.S!

- Y for 'yawn' to open up your breathing.

- E for 'easy' and finding ease and pleasure within your throat.

- S.S.S.S.S.S! for 'stretch' 'shoulders' 'snake' 'spinal stretch' 'sigh' 'smile' 'sing/slide' – and more 's's for: 'shower songs' 'soft songs' 'silly songs' 'sexy songs' 'sultry songs' . . .

Summary of Part Two

- Your body is the 'ground' for all your feelings, thoughts – and songs.

- Anatomy helps us locate different body structures in relation to each other.

- Every structure concerned with the creating of vocal sound can be influenced through a combination of thought, imagination and muscular action.

- All muscles have three basic actions according to what we require from them: they stretch, contract and relax.

- How we hold ourselves affects the sound of our songs.

- Better breathing begins in the backbone.

- Stretching open the whole jaw to yawn or laugh is one of the pleasures of life. Mobility in the jaw is vital to all vocalising.

- Singing is all about a magical relationship with the air we breathe.

- The diaphragm is the largest single muscle in the body and is the main muscle of respiration.

- Our breathing patterns are strongly influenced by our feelings.

- The vocal folds are muscles with the power to vibrate, transforming breath into sound waves.

- All muscles develop with use and weaken or become rigid without use. All muscles will get more and more responsive with practice and training. Remember how birds and small children repeat and repeat? And repeat.

- Our ears hear and *feel* sound.

Voice: Mind, Heart, Body and . . . Sound

'My love to thee is sound, sans crack or flaw.'
William Shakespeare, *Love's Labour's Lost*, V.ii

Voice: Mind, Heart, Body and . . . Sound

Vibration and Resonance – Making Sound

Many people, when asked to say where their voice comes from, will point to their neck, and insist that their voice is made in their throat. But, as we have learned, what goes on in the throat is only part of the story. For the vibration created in the vocal folds to carry, it must be resonated by other structures around it. To develop the full vibrant sound of your own voice, you must now explore body structures from a new viewpoint.

Vocal sound results from a combination of breath, vibration and resonance. Resonance is what makes a voice 'ring', and gives it clarity. We are aware of this all the time, not just when we are singing, or listening to someone else's singing, but also when we speak. Without the effects of resonance, the sound of our voices would be thin and muffled, reduced to not much more than a whisper.

A NEW SUBSTANCE

In this section it will be helpful to think not so much of 'voice' but of breath turned into sound waves – this will be referred to as the 'Vibrating Out-Breath': VOB. The amazing transformation of breath into sound – the 'making' of sound – is similar to the way the food we eat is transformed into energy and heat. Breath goes in, and comes out as something different from just breath. This simple observation emphasises the need to give attention to the in-breath, as much as to the sound we make. In much the same way that oxygen is 'food' for fire, and music is the 'food' of love, breath is 'food' to vocal sound.

*Resonance is the happy result
of the meeting between VOB and matter.*

RAISING YOUR VOICE

If there is resonance in our speaking voices, it will be there when we sing. It is heightened when we raise our voices, or shout. To 'raise' the voice simply means to make closer contact, through the out-going breath, with the upper fields of resonance within the skull; we literally 'raise' the vibrating breath higher – just as we raise our voices in song.

As your out-breath rises upwards through the lungs and larynx, the inside of your head will be the first and most important centre of resonance. Close your lips lightly and make a light humming sound, holding your cupped hands over your ears at the same time. Your entire head seems to be abuzz with sound. With your lips still lightly together, press the tip of your tongue firmly to the roof of your mouth as you hum, making a NNNNN sound: this will accentuate the resonance.

SKULLS, CAVES, CAVERNS, CATHEDRALS AND DOMES

It is equally possible for a single voice, unaided by artificial amplification, to fill an entire cathedral or temple, and for a whisper or sigh to fill a very small Romanesque chapel. The domes, ceilings and vaulted arches of most ancient buildings were specially constructed to catch and amplify the harmonics of vocal and instrumental sound. Stone and bone have similar capacities for both vibrating and resonating sound vibration. This is known as 'bone conduction'. The skull has its own internal miniature domes and vaults, making it as full of 'resonating chambers' as the temple, cathedral or chapel.

A HOLE IN THE HEAD

The important thing for us to know about the head in relation to resonance is that its hard structure is essentially hollow. There are areas inside the head that function as free passageways for the air we breathe, filtering it and warming it. These are the inter-connecting spaces between throat, nose and mouth. Even when we fill our mouths with food, or when we drink, the back of the throat remains open for the passage of air. If you don't believe this, take a mouthful of water and hold it in your mouth while breathing in and out through your nose at the same time!

You can even hum with the water in your mouth. In fact it is only while swallowing that the air passages are closed off, by the epiglottis (the little flap that closes over the glottis).

The inside of your mouth (10–15 seconds)

Sit with your elbows resting on a table and put your cheekbones forwards into your hands, letting your mouth 'hang open' for a moment. With your tongue resting against the teeth of your lower jaw, breathe easily and allow yourself to become aware of the shape of your mouth. Your tongue creates the 'floor' of this space; the hard palate, the 'roof'. Can you imagine the shape of the roof of your mouth? Can you feel the inside of your cheeks? Can you feel the back of your throat, or the space behind your nose? Imagine Jonah standing just inside the whale's open mouth and having a look around. Relax. Breathe. Shake, 'snake' your shoulders.

Resonance, MMO and the 'echo effect'

The more mobile and open we can make the space inside our mouths, the more effectively the sound will resonate. We have our own 'oral echo chamber' inside the mouth — think of the noise made just by crunching a piece of toast! To appreciate the resonating capacities of the interior of your mouth, take an in-breath, hold it, keeping your lips open, and then make clicking sounds with your tongue: CLIP-CLOP. Breathe normally again. Repeat with your lips closed, listening to the difference in the sound you make. Cover and uncover your ears to listen. You could blow out your cheeks and tap them with your fingers, make popping sounds by hooking your finger inside your cheek and then releasing it, or make loud kissing sounds — exaggerate! The sounds you make do not come up from the lungs through the larynx on the VOB, but are solely the echo effect within the resonating space, resulting from a meeting of matter and substance. Making such sounds are good exercise for your tongue and lips as well.

The roof of the mouth or hard palate (1 minute)

You may need to have a handkerchief handy for this exploratory exercise! Put your right or left thumb into your mouth, just like you did as a child, and gently explore the roof, or hard palate, of your mouth. Just feel what is there: the shape and contours. Take care not to explore too far back or you will make contact with the soft part at the back (the soft palate), which feels uncomfortable because it is very sensitive to foreign objects, such as your thumb, coming too far inside the mouth.

The shape is not flat, as you may have imagined, but feels rounded and domed. This domed shape offers more open space to resonate the sound waves of your out-going breath.

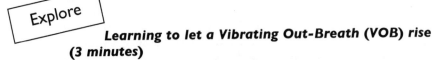

Learning to let a Vibrating Out-Breath (VOB) rise (3 minutes)

- Relax the lower jaw, letting it hang; bring your tongue forward and feel the tip just inside your lower teeth.

- Breathe in, using vowel sounds AAAH or OHHH. Then concentrate on letting the VOB *rise* into the 'vaults' of your hard palate. Think of filling these 'vaults' with sound. Notice what happens to the pitch of sound. Can you raise the VOB without raising or changing the pitch?

- Without forcing, do this again, paying attention to your in-breath and widening your ribs to sustain the sound.

- Repeat.

Learning to direct sound

You can gradually learn to direct the out-going breath into different parts of the mouth, with exciting effects on the sound.

- Relax, open your jaw and let your tongue rest in the bottom of your mouth.

- Breathe in.

- Focusing on the vaulted shape of the roof of the mouth, allow your VOB to rise on an open vowel sound, such as AAAH or OOOH.

- If your sound is breathy or rough, you are probably pushing air, or you are breathing too much in your throat, at the level of the 'false cords'.

- Create sound by allowing the transformation from breath into VOB to take place naturally, as a result of your mental direction.

- Breathe in as and when you need to.

- Keep your whole face and body alert, mobile and responsive to the direction of the sound.

- You can now try to 'move' the sound about as it flows out of your mouth:

  Towards the front upper teeth.

  Towards the middle of the 'vault'.

  Towards the back of the throat.

With practice, this exercise will allow you to experience the whole surface area of the hard palate, from front to back and vice-versa. Observe how the pitch and tone colour changes: the sound seems deeper the more you direct the VOB to the back of the hard palate, and higher as you bring it forward. Should you experience tickling sensations in the back of your throat, this probably means that you are pushing the sound, rather than letting it rise. You need less effort, more focus. Try a softer sound to begin with.

Resonance from inside the head – bone conduction (5 minutes)

The skull, as we know, is bone, providing a firm, protective shell for the brain. The roof of the mouth is actually part of the base of the skull. Since bone conducts sound, it follows that the more of the base of the skull's surface area we can contact with our Vibrating Out-Breath, the more resonance we are likely to achieve throughout the skull. This is one of the reasons for aiming for an open, expanded, yawning in-breath.

- In an upright sitting position, breathe in and out with your mouth open and your jaw relaxed. Repeat this a few times with your eyes closed.

- Imagine the dome-shaped roof of your mouth getting bigger and rounder; feel the connection with your body.

- Make yourself a mental image of the dome of the diaphragm inside the base of your ribs, the dome of the hard palate, and the dome of your skull. Close your eyes.

- Try and imagine that the upper domes are as large as the lower one.

- Feel the breath circulating through your head and lungs. Feel the expansion in your ribs, and the rising and falling of your breath. Yawn to increase the space even more. You might begin to feel like a huge breathing egg.

- Be careful not to let all the muscles of your face sag, even though your jaw is relaxed and open.

- Make sound, play, vocalise, sing. Do-be-do-be-do-BE.

- Repeat the entire exercise, this time in different ways: in a satisfied way, a questioning one, with longing, or with affection. Notice how the sound changes as you change the message.

RESONATING THE WHOLE BODY

At this point it is important to realise that the vocal folds set in vibration the breath *below* them, as well as the breath going through them: it is all part of the same flow of air. The breath that is still inside the body, as well as the outgoing breath, will vibrate – as does the air all around us. Through activating the fields of resonance, we thus surround ourselves, both inside and out, with a whole field of vibration.

Explore

Fields of resonance

Let a Vibrating Out-Breath, on an open vowel sound – AAAAH – rise easily from your lungs through your larynx and make contact with the entire roof of your mouth as it leaves your body. Don't push the air. Trust the flow of air: think MMO (Muscles, Mobility, Openness). Make yourself a mental image of the vibrations rolling out of your mouth, your ears, your eyes and the entire surface of your head, right down your spine and on to your feet. Keep the sound waves in motion through steady in-breaths and out-breaths, and set in motion the air around your entire body.

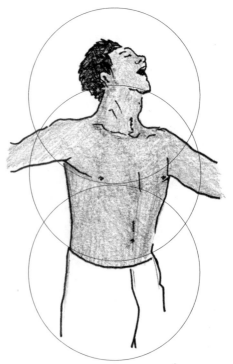

The circles of vibration.

Singing with wide-open eyes

Keep your eyes wide open as you slide/sing easily up and down, raising and lowering the pitch of your voice without forcing it. From the middle part of your voice, make a NAH or low YEAH sound that you can feel in your chest, and 'think' the sound as you sing/slide, up and under and then over the domed roof of your mouth, right into the spaces behind your eyes, 'opening' the upper space to your sound.

OPENING UP THE ROOF: DISCOVERING THE SOFT PALATE

When you laugh wildly, you may reveal to others, if not to yourself, something interesting at the back of your throat. This is a muscular flap, known as the soft palate, at the back of the roof of the mouth, or hard palate. If you explore this area by putting your thumb far back in your mouth, you will almost certainly be sick. The flap is like a little 'curtain' that hangs above the back of the mouth, separating and protecting the nasal passageways. It can move either up or down. The soft palate's function is to discourage us from cramming too much food too far back in our throat. When there is no food in our mouth, this little flap appears to serve no particular purpose. It plays a big role in the direction of air in and out of the mouth and nose, however, and therefore helps the direction of resonance. Some researchers have been examining the role of this little flap in snoring problems.

Explore

Curtain up and curtain down – the sound of snoring

- First, experiment by making a few of your own snoring noises, and then try to locate where and how the sound is made, and which muscles, also useful for singing, are used.

- Pinch your nose, open your mouth and think of dropping the 'curtain' down at the back of your mouth over the back of your tongue: try to breathe in. You will probably make a snoring noise! This will tell you immediately that if you want air to pass through your mouth, the 'curtain', or soft palate, will have to be raised.

- Repeat. Pinch your nose, but think of raising the curtain. Breathe in. This time, no snoring!

To allow more space for your in-breath and the outgoing VOB, you must therefore 'raise the curtain'.

This exercise might help snorers, as well as singers, strengthen this useful little muscle.

- Experiment by directing breath either through your mouth or through your nose. Hold your fingers beneath your nose, or in front of your mouth, and feel the moist breath as you change the direction of your airflow.

- Decide whether the 'curtain' is up or down when you hum.

- Sing/slide E-I-E-I-O, either with your nose pinched or without. Feel the difference. Decide which gives the most resonance to your voice.

N.B. The soft palate, in the relaxed position, is neither 'up' nor 'down', and allows the passage of air between both mouth and nose.

Sounds nosy (5 minutes)

At one time or another most of us have had the experience of 'talking' through our noses. We have this familiar-sounding voice when we have a cold, or an adenoidal condition, or we can produce it playfully, as a joke. You can easily find this area of resonance at the back of your nose by lifting either the back or the tip of your tongue against the roof of your mouth, thus directing all the out-going stream of air through your nose. With the air-stream effectively blocked off from your mouth, make a sound on NNNNNN, then with a percussive: NA-NA-NA.

Alternatively, pronounce the sound UNG. This will lift the back of your tongue up against the back of the soft palate and achieve the same effect of directing the air-stream out through your nostrils. SUNG. LUNG. RUNG.

Long-nosed witches

One of the easiest ways to take the outgoing stream of air into your head is to imagine yourself with a witch's very long, pointed and inquisitive nose. With this image in mind, begin to make little nasty, nosy, witch-like sounds. They will probably be quite high. Think them as far forwards as you can. Give witch-like chuckles up in your nose: TEE-HEE-HEE! You will be surprised at the amount of energy you release simply by expressing these 'wicked witch' sounds. They have a completely different feel from the sounds you achieved by opening up the whole of the roof of your mouth – they are possibly more full of character, and less 'musical'.

Explore the different kinds of resonance you can find by moving the sound stream around between your nose and mouth with your tongue and soft palate, and by adopting different facial expressions. Remember that the eyes affect sound too. Notice what happens when they are either wide-open or squeezed tight shut.

RESONATING 'BODIES'

To get an idea of sound resonating, lean against a piano when someone is playing, or put your hands onto a friend's back and shoulders lightly while they are speaking or singing. Notice the effect of vibrations of highly amplified dance music on your body.

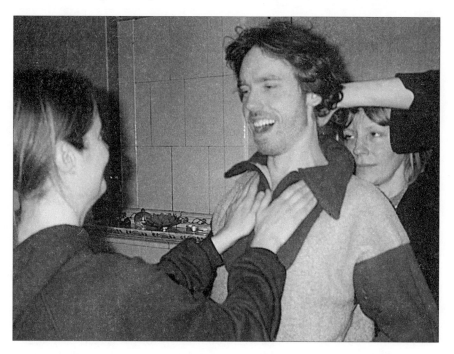

Resonance, the meeting of matter and substance, varies according to:

- The size, shape and density of the matter – in this case, body structures.

- The speed, volume and pressure of the sound waves – in this case, your VOB.

Think of a large bronze gong, first struck by an enormous hammer, and then bumped into accidentally by a small fluffy dog – the first sound is far more resonant than the second. The first sound is like that made by a high-pressure VOB, made with a clear intention for contact and communication, that creates high resonance; the unresonant sound of the fluffy dog bumping into the gong is like that produced by a wobbly, low-pressure, unfocused out-breath.

Every gong, or drum, however large or small, has a 'power centre' that, if struck, results in the maximum amount of resonance being liberated. The human body has similar 'power centres' for resonance. The most obvious one is the head itself. The 'object' for striking the 'power centre' is your VOB, directed by a clear intention.

Resonant greetings

Even the fluffy dog can contact centres of resonance vibrantly – by barking. You can also try barking to explore heightened resonance, which can then be taken into your singing voice. Start with a little gentle yapping. Then give it an intention – greeting or warning: yap-yap-yap, and then YAP! YAP! YOW! YOW! Remember to direct the VOB upwards, letting it rise into the roof of the mouth. Think high and open, as opera singers do. You will feel a movement in the throat as the larynx rises. Did you feel the diaphragm muscles at work? You are using the same effort as when you are coughing, keeping the throat wide open – a power punch at 600mph!

Resonance within the body

- Make yourself a mental image of the passage of your breath as it moves in and out through your nostrils, into the back of your throat, your larynx and into your chest.

- Smile with your little 'inner lips'. Start up a light humming sound, adjusting the pitch of sound from low to high so that it feels easy and you can keep making it without strain in your throat. Remember the 'three keys' in your spine, think about alignment, aim for openness to allow sound vibrations to circulate through your body.

- Every now and then, place your hands lightly over your upper chest.

- Breathe in when you need to, widening the lower ribs to 'hold' out the diaphragm, thus slowing down your out-breath to prolong and support your sound.

- When the sound is coming, play lightly with pitch and volume by humming or gently voicing higher or lower, louder or softer – as you wish. Imagine all this as the little fluffy dog snuffling around . . . or as though you were gently sounding over the surface of a special gong.

- Stretch. Uncurl, roll, wriggle, bend, swing your arms, take an arm-swinging walk to a place and space, either inside or out, where you can make a loud resonant sound without embarrassment.

Going for the BIG SOUND

'One of these mornin's you're goin' to rise up singin'.'
Ira Gershwin, 'Summertime', from *Porgy and Bess*, 1935

Wake up and warm up with the arm/shoulder/spine 'snake' exercise and back of the neck stretches.

You will need to find an open or soundproofed space where you can let your voice out.

Now you are going to try and 'hit the centre of the gong'. Where will the power come from? VOB, along with a clear intention. Give yourself a reason. Remember PVE. We use high resonating loud sounds for particular reasons: to be heard far away; to attract attention; to express extremes of joy, anger or pain; to warn or to alert; to sell our wares in the market. Think of other reasons why you might want to call out or yell.

To yell or call without intent, real or imagined, is to create confusion in the body.

Whether acted or 'real', your motivation represents at least half the power of the sound.

- Hear the sound of your call in your imagination fully before you express it.

- The image/reason/feeling/intention will take care of the smaller vocal muscles – you will remember to prepare the larger structures for effort.

- Take a 'hungry' in-breath. With a really wide-open yawning jaw, let the whole body gulp in a huge mouthful of air.

- Let your in-breath expand your whole rib cage, keeping your lower ribs wide.

- Then, without pausing, give voice on a full open NNNNAAAAOOOOH! NOW! Or YAA- AYEE! Or FIRE! – FAAYAAH!

- Or WHAHAYEEE? Or HEEYAA-AYE-AAAM!

- Make the connection between your centre and all the space you've discovered above it: let the sound project – call! Think of Tarzan, or of Liza Minnelli, underneath the railway bridge in the film *Cabaret*. But go one better: allow the power for your breath to rise from your centre, your plexus; think down to below the diaphragm and let the VOB make direct unhindered contact with the entire surface of the roof of your mouth and back of your throat.

- Repeat. *Less pressure, more space.*

- Allow your breath to carry the sound-waves into and through the resonating centres of your skull, and thus, through bone conduction, into your entire body. Go for the big sound. Once you've found it, follow the sound. Make it again. Sing it out. Enjoy your in-breath.

- Repeat. *More focus, less effort.*

- Relax. By reducing the pressure around your throat you will contact more resonance. Trust your voice to follow your intention. It will, if the intention is clear. If you felt anything catch or tickle in your throat, you may need to go back and re-read the previous sections and repeat the earlier exercises. If your voice came out loud and free, you've got the message. Let the VOB rise from your centre.

RESONANCE AND VOLUME

Resonance, by bringing out 'harmonics' (explained later in this section), immediately amplifies a sound, however small. A resonant sound 'carries'; it has a clarity and 'ring' that is very different from a sound pushed into high volume by muscular strain from below. You may have had the experience, while singing in the bath, of finding a frequency in your voice that seems to set the entire bathroom booming – with no effort at all. Acoustic science is partly about finding architectural structures that amplify different frequencies. The most important thing to discover about resonance is that you can contact and develop it to give colour, nuance and meaning to all your vocal expression.

SINGING FROM THE HEART

This is where mind and feeling come together through the body. We can learn, through using our breath, to activate the 'heart energies' and send them out into sound.

If you remember that the vocal folds set the whole out-going air-stream into vibration, you will not be surprised to feel vibration and resonance in your upper chest – and around your heart as well. In fact, the vibration spreads around the entire chest from front to back as it is set into vibration. When the vibration is focused around the heart, it is as though the heart muscle itself warms and expands, creating a new feeling and a deeper vibration. Singing class students enjoy the exercise of 'listening in' to the vibrations of chest and heart resonance, which sometimes seems to evoke early memories of listening to sound through water in the womb during pregnancy.

Finding heart resonance (5 to 10 minutes)

- Place your hands over and above your heart. This time, instead of taking the sound up into the roof of your mouth, think of keeping it very lightly just on or below your tongue – not your throat. Sing/slide lightly from high to low until you find a tone that 'sits' easily. You will soon feel light vibrations of sound in your heart area.

- Place an imaginary 'mouth' below your throat in the upper chest, and imagine that you can sing through that second, lower mouth.

- In a forward-sitting position that allows you to move your back and expand on the in-breath, search for the smallest, most tender and gentle sound you are capable of finding.

- Take your time. Give yourself time for your in-breath. Slow down and make hardly any effort at all, without pushing out the air, or straining.

- Sing/slide gently through the middle part of your voice until you find this soft, clear sound. You will know it when you find it, because it pulses together with your heartbeat and you can feel the warmth of your out-breath.

- Feel the warmth of this sound; listen to the colour of the sound, repeating it again and again so that you will never lose the ability, however brilliant your upper resonance, or 'head sounds', to sing from the heart.

Singing the sound out from head and heart (10 minutes)

Make yourself as aware as possible of the resonating spaces in mouth and chest; sing on the word 'younger', pronounce it as YOUNGAH!

Remember :

1 The UNG sound you found to place your breath behind your nose.

2 The openness you found to reach the upper resonators.

3 The open AAAH sound with which you contacted the body resonance in your upper chest and heart.

- Sing YOUNGAH and YOUNGAAAH!

- Once you have been able to differentiate between the two fields of resonance, try opening up to one and not the other.

- Try placing all the resonance in and above the dome of your mouth – or, conversely, focusing the vibration and resonance in the chest around, above and below your heart, especially by expanding and widening the ribs. Notice the different quality of sound as you move the out-going air-stream from one field to another.

Alternating fields of resonance

- Sing up and down your accessible pitch range on E-I-E-I-O, with an easy playful feeling. Expand and sustain any of the different vowel sounds: EE AAYEE OOO.

- Then try and alternate the two fields: the lower one to give you depth and feeling, the upper one to give your voice vibrancy and 'ring'.

- Now try and join the two fields – upper and lower.

- Enjoy the fullness of your sound. Don't worry if you swoop around; you're not training, you are exploring.

- Just for fun, try to imagine taking the sound into other parts of your body than just your head or chest.

- Explore possibilities in an illogical way! Could you make your ankles vibrate? Or sing into your elbows?

AIR POWER AND FIELDS OF RESONANCE

Remember:

1   A power supply – the mind/body relationship to breath.

2   A vibrating centre – the vocal folds in the larynx.

3   Resonating fields – the head and the body.

Practise any of the exercises in this section again, this time basing them on what you have discovered in Part Two before going on to the practical exercises of the next section.

The Harmonics of Sound

'The leading theory of how the universe could have exploded out of the primordial nothingness, known as the theory of inflation, predicts that the quantum fluctuations should have rattled the universe in such a way that it resonated like a vast organ pipe, with one main tone, or wavelength, and a series of overtones or harmonics. An old (and colossal) song.'

James Glanz, *New York Times*, 2 May 2001

BREAKING FREE FROM GRAVITY AND TIME

There is a particular pitch or range of sound for each individual, which, when they encounter it, enables them to experience their voice suddenly as 'spinning' free. It is unmistakable when you find it. You will experience a very clear, warm, shining tone that, however small, seems to 'ring' and expand far beyond the confines of your skull. It may feel almost disembodied, as though it is floating somewhere above or around you: sound, after all, is not subject to gravity. This special tone may be a bit like the sound you make when you rub the wet rim of a wine glass – like Pythagoras apparently did, while exploring the harmonics of sound in the fifth century BC. This tone seems to have an extraordinarily clear musical resonance. Once you discover it, you can find it again and again through your kinetic (muscular) and auditory (listening) memory.

'Harmonics is the DNA of musical sound.'
David Hykes, founder of the Harmonic Chant

As your listening ability sharpens, you may begin to hear extra notes, over and above the main one that is being sung. The main note is called the fundamental, or base note. The other notes that surround it, and give it brilliance and 'ring', are known as harmonics. This crystalline quality that harmonics give the voice is not unique to the human species. We can hear a similar quality of 'pure' sound in the 'songs' of dolphins, whales and birds, and they, as well as us, are now known to 'play' with this particular musical quality in the voice and 'compose' their own meaningful songs.

RIPPLES OF SOUND

The image of a stone flung into a pool of water may help you to understand what is going on. The first ripple, appearing as the stone meets the water, represents the fundamental note, and the expanding circles of ripples it creates around it are like the harmonics of a single tone. The number of ripples formed relates to the size and depth of the pool. In the same way, the number of harmonics perceived depends on the resonating space and upon the hearing capacity of the listener. For instance, if a pin is dropped onto the marble floor directly under the dome of St Paul's Cathedral in London, some people may hear it and others may not. Some people may hear the sound very faintly; some, with acute hearing, might even be shocked by the sound! The reverberations of the pin-drop will go spinning off into space until they meet something dense or solid to stop them resonating further. The idea that every single sound made goes on forever, echoing into infinity – 'the music of the spheres' – is linked to this idea of the endless 'rippling' of sound.

Sound contains a spectrum of harmonics
just as light contains a rainbow spectrum of colours.

The harmonic spectrum of each fundamental, or base note, is accentuated, shaped or enlarged by whatever vessel, whether human or instrumental, is 'sounded'.

OVERTONE SINGING

Overtone singing is a meditative form of singing that develops the ability to accentuate all or any of the harmonics of the fundamental note sung. The sounds it produces are fascinating to listen to, and can have a calming and almost hypnotic effect on the listener and the singer, rather like the very first singing sounds we ever made. Meditative toning, or chanting, over a prolonged period of time is known to bring about a state of calm and tranquillity. Because of the need to establish calm and steady breathing, and the way in which the VOB is set into motion and resonates, overtone chanting is an excellent preparation for all kinds of singing, as well as being a joyful experience in itself.

Although the very best and most enjoyable way to learn overtone singing is with a teacher or a group, all the exercises suggested so far will provide you with a good base, and the following exploration will help you make or confirm your own discoveries.

Explore

The 'Hourglass': exploring overtones
(30 minutes)

- Arms/shoulder/spine 'snake' exercise, to warm through the body.

- Sit comfortably in an upright position.

- Massage your face, yawning as you do so; massage your scalp, making your hair move; massage behind your ears and the back of your neck.

- Imagine the shape of a large soft 'hourglass' into your body. Imagine it made not of glass, but of a soft, expandable, transparent material that fills up with your breath.

- As you breathe in, imagine filling up the lower globe, visualising it as somewhere below the neck.

- As you breathe out, imagine the air moving through the narrow neck of the hourglass and filling up the upper globe, visualising it as somewhere in your head.

- Start a gentle humming in the middle of your vocal range, seeking a pitch of sound that vibrates clearly inside your mouth.

- Still humming, imagine that you can now move or direct the VOB up or down into the space at the back of your lips, over your tongue and the back of your throat and into the roof of your mouth. Yawn when you need to, and continue.

- Breathe in through your nose. Let each sound easily, gently and progressively fill the inside of your mouth as the VOB rises from your throat. You don't need to push. Just open wide the back of your throat on the preparatory in-breath.

- Repeat as if you were actually filling your mouth with water, until you can clearly feel your vocal vibration filling the entire inside of your mouth and beyond your skull. Breathe in, through your nose, when necessary.

- Keep bringing the sound up from your throat on the VOB, and then into your mouth, like water from a well, widening and expanding the 'globe' inside your mouth as much as possible.

- Relax the jaw and let the lips open slightly. Shape a sound between an O and an AW. Change the pitch of sound, or make soft siren sounds to help you explore the upper 'globe'.

- Do you feel the roof of your mouth now? Is the sound ringing in your ears? Did the sound suddenly become more 'free' than when it was in your throat?

- Breathe in when necessary, giving the image time to establish itself in your mind.

Reversing the 'Hourglass'

- Now reverse the process. Move the sound from your mouth into the 'lower' globe. This involves singing a lower pitch of sound.

- As you do this, keep an awareness of the 'three keys' in your spine: keep energy circulating between them by moving each key area gently as you work.

- Visualise the globes expanding all the time, and visualise the sound passing through the neck passage downwards into the lower globe.

- With your lips apart, set the out-going breath into sound vibration on the vowel O as in 'go' – directing the sound into the lower globe. You will achieve a deep or low sound that vibrates behind the breastbone. Put your fingers on your chest to feel the vibrations.

- With the next VOB begin to sing/slide gently from the lower 'globe' up into the higher 'globe'. Remember – MMO. Expand!

- Let the sound slide easily up from your chest and into your mouth.

- Keeping the feeling and sound in the upper globe (in your mouth) on your VOB, begin to make the sound OO – EE – O – EE. Breathe in when you need to, expanding and widening the ribs fully.

Using the tongue to direct the Vibrating Out-Breath

- Keeping the inside of your mouth as fully expanded as you can, let the very tip of your tongue come up towards the roof of the mouth to shape the EE sound, as though inside or within the O. In doing this, you narrow the passageway for air and direct the VOB to a small area of the roof of the mouth and to the back of the nasal passages.

- Sing/sound the EE lightly and freely up and down, between both 'globes' of head and body, alternating with the deeper O sound – on the same breath. You will eventually hear at least two clear sounds in your voice at one and the same time. You may even have the joy of hearing a harmonic 'singing free', seemingly above your head.

- Trust your auditory and kinetic memory to store the sensations you experienced. A new sound, like a new idea, is never forgotten.

Singing in Tune

To cultivate an awareness of all sound as vibration, however small, is to return to the natural relationship with sound that we had as infants. It is the starting point for rediscovering the ability to 'sing on the note' and 'sing in tune'.

The phrase 'singing in tune' should really be 'singing in tune with someone or something'. If you are singing a tune or melody of your own invention, on your own, there is never any problem, since no one knows the melody except you, and no one can say whether you are 'in tune' or not. You could be singing very advanced atonal music, or just simple but unknown little tunes. Take note, and take heart. Tone deaf doesn't mean daft – it can mean just highly original! However, when you want to sing with other people, or you want to sing someone else's melody, then you have to learn to sing 'in tune'. It is rather like learning to know the difference between your right and left foot so that you can fall into step with someone else's rhythm.

RELAXATION AND LISTENING:
THE PLANE, THE HAMMER AND THE KETTLE

Singing in tune and falling in step with a rhythm both come more easily the more relaxed you are. The more relaxed your body, the more easily it will receive and respond to the vibration. The vibration we receive easily is related immediately, and without distortion, to the sound source it came from. Thus we immediately recognise the droning of a distant plane, the banging of a hammer, the whistling of a kettle, and so on. No one has ever insisted that we sing the exact pitch of the droning plane, banging hammer or whistling kettle, but we perceive quite clearly and effortlessly the difference in sound vibration and pitch.

A tense and anxious person trying desperately to 'listen', by an effort of will, is actually closing him/herself off to sound vibration. Exhortations to 'Listen properly!' will never work, because they induce either stress or panic, both enemies to this kind of listening, and generally set up a vicious circle of despair and resistance which takes time to undo.

An understanding of how we make vocal sound, together with a new approach to hearing sound as vibration with the whole body, will, for most people, remove the 'block' and restore the natural ear/voice connection.

Remember: The link between the ears and the back of the throat is such that every sound we perceive is also felt, and responded to, as vibration within the larynx.

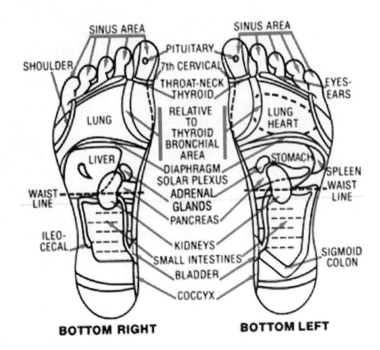

BOTTOM RIGHT   **BOTTOM LEFT**

Develop

Listening from the soles of your feet: cultivating auditory awareness (at least 20 minutes)

The long-established practice of reflexology recognises that the entire nervous system is reflected in the soles of the feet. Even without much knowledge, you can discover that by massaging your feet you will directly relax and benefit the rest of your body. There are many books on the subject, and they are well worth studying. For now, find a bottle of massage oil or similar – add aromatherapy oils, if you have them – and select one of your favourite calm and gentle pieces of music on tape or CD. Instrumental music is best for this exercise: listen to woodwind, keyboard, drums, percussion or strings – something to take your mind off voice for a while!

Find a quiet and cosy corner to relax in, undisturbed.

* Find a comfortable sitting or lying-down position. Take one of your feet between both hands and give it a good all-over rub, using the massage oil. Stop and stretch out your back whenever you need to, then continue. Give yourself time to massage your feet lovingly, especially the toes – they don't often get such attention, especially not in voice-training sessions!

- After massaging one foot, stretch out on your back. Close your eyes and give yourself time to appreciate the difference of feeling between the foot you have massaged and the other one. This feeling may well spread up the entire leg or the entire side of the body. You will feel differences in size, temperature and weight. Rest for a while and listen to the music.

- Massage the other foot in the same way as the first, stretching out your back when you need to. When you have massaged both feet, turn off the music.

- Lie down on your back, with your knees bent and your feet flat on the floor. Rest your head on a pillow if you need to. Close your eyes and listen, both inwardly and outwardly. What do you hear? What is the highest pitch of sound you can hear? The lowest? Can you feel the sound? Listen again. How many sounds can you hear? Can you separate them from each other? Can you feel your own heartbeat at the same time? Do you enjoy the sounds you hear, or are you consciously or unconsciously trying to block them off? Maybe you need to block some off to listen to the others, but be aware of what you are doing. Let every sound vibration travel through you: in one ear and out the other. Listen with your eyes closed. Listen with your eyes open. Try to distinguish between high sounds and low sounds, loud and soft or sharp and dull ones. Observe what happens to your breathing as you listen. Do you feel any movement in your larynx as you listen? Can you imagine yourself imitating the sounds you hear?

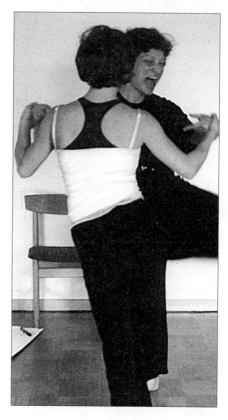

- Stretch out your back. Wriggle, roll over on your side, yawn, uncurl, get back on your feet, put the music back on – something new, something rhythmic and upbeat – dance to the rhythm, dance to the beat, use your feet, move your body. Feel the vibrations. Sing along. Trust your voice to fall in tune.

Once you begin to sharpen your awareness of the sounds all around you, you are ready to trust the ear/voice connection and sing 'in tune'.

SINGING 'ON THE NOTE'

Every sound we hear represents a 'frequency' of vibration, or a 'pitch'. A frequency refers to the rate of vibrations per second. The slower the vibration, the lower the frequency; the faster the vibration, the higher the frequency – right up to those frequencies only audible to bats and butterflies.

If you have been following the previous sections actively you will already have gained a good idea of where to find high, middle and low sounds in your voice. You will have begun to develop that most important of skills: a kinaesthetic, or 'physical awareness' of sound. The main objective has been to develop an awareness of the link between breath and body in the creation of sound.

FROM HIGH TO LOW

The previous exercises have been designed to allow you to explore freely, letting your voice slide, swoop, soar and hum, without tying it down to any particular shape, form or pitch. In this way, you have become aware of the natural movement in the voice from low to high, which is there for you to find – you do not have to learn it, simply to rediscover it and follow it. It is this natural sequence from high to middle and low sounds that we have been playing with since babyhood and on which all music is based. As you sing/slide, you are unconsciously learning that one tone leads to another – the one closest to it, either up or down. You begin to hear and get used to the natural vocal movement towards higher tones or towards lower tones. To refresh your memory, do a bit of 'musical yawning', and notice the natural cadenzas (elaborate flourishes) you sing!

SELECTING A FREQUENCY

In making the 'sing/slide/siren' sound from the top to the bottom of your voice, the sound passes through many different frequencies. It is a bit like turning the tuning knob of a radio through all the stations without stopping. You get an idea of the range of frequencies available, but you don't actually pick up the news programme. To hear the 'news', you need to stop and select one frequency from your voice at a time. This is where a musical instrument can help.

The piano, for instance, can be used as a tool to help you to stop at any frequency in your range, and 'tune' your voice in – not only to the musical note, but also more acutely to different qualities hidden within your voice at any particular frequency.

Working with a Piano

Everyone has a voice, but not everyone has a piano. In fact, many people not only do not have a piano but are actually nervous, unsure or even scared of what pianos might reveal about their voice and their ability to sing. This section is essentially for you, the 'piano-phobes'.

Access to a piano does not imply access to (or knowledge of) your voice. You may have 'transferred' your voice to your instrument – it has a 'voice', but your own singing voice is masked or muted. Both piano-phobes and musicians can benefit from using the piano as a support for their vocal development, and piano-phobes in particular can learn to let the piano guide them towards musical structure.

OVERCOMING PIANO-PHOBIA

The piano has a great advantage in that you do not have to learn to play it in order to use it. The piano will help you develop both the ear/voice connection and the musical qualities in your voice. No matter how much or how little you know about musical sound, if you press a key on the piano you will hear the pitch of sound that you are supposed to hear (for a normal, tuned piano, of course). It won't be an approximation, vaguely where you expected it, a little sharp or flat, and so on, but exactly what it always is: a Middle C, for example. If you then press down the key right next to it you will hear exactly half a tone higher, or lower; a semi-tone. You can rely on that. The piano gives you easy-to-find and precise tones and half-tones.

> *'Blue Moon, now I'm no longer alone,*
> *Without a dream in my heart,*
> *Without a love of my own.'*

> Lorenz Hart, 'Blue Moon', 1934

It is sometimes difficult to work on your voice when on your own, but once you have a piano, or keyboard, you are no longer alone. The piano gives you a measure for your voice.

A keyboard of any kind, either acoustic or electronic, will be useful. A traditional piano keyboard has a range of seven octaves; your piano or electronic keyboard should have at least five. With five octaves you will easily cover the full range of your voice and still have a few notes left over to entice you into non-musical, simply human areas. If you cannot get hold of a keyboard immediately, then for the sake of your vocal development and pleasure, investigate the possibility of either borrowing a friend's piano or keyboard or renting a music studio with a piano – at least once.

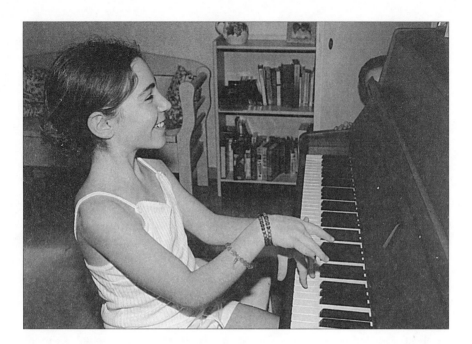

A FIRST RENDEZVOUS WITH YOUR VOICE AT THE PIANO

Once you have found, begged, borrowed, rented, bought or otherwise acquired a keyboard, and found the right space to practise it, you're ready to begin – how does it feel? Here you are, neither a singer nor a pianist, on your own in front of a lot of inscrutable black and white piano keys that seem already to know more than you do. How are you going to break the silence? How are you going to overcome your embarrassment? To sing for others is sometimes bad enough, but the first time one makes a special rendezvous with only oneself, it can be even worse. How will you know whether or not you are just wasting your time? How will you know whether what you do is any good?

Your voice at the piano (10–20 minutes)

The following exploratory exercises are suggested as ways of helping you 'break the ice'.

Can you imagine a cat jumping onto the keyboard? Can you see it tiptoeing gingerly along the keys? Plinkety-plonk, plink, plink, plink? It doesn't matter how hesitantly you start, the geography of the keyboard is yours to explore.

- Start yawning and stretching like a cat to open up your body and voice as you do so. Sing a few 'hour-glass' sounds from your chest up to your head and down again.

- Explore the difference between the black and white keys; play all the white ones from the left to the right and back again from right to left, one by one.

- Then play all the black ones. It doesn't matter which fingers. Use all your fingers or just one. There is no right or wrong way in this exploration.

- Do what is easiest. Run the back of your hand up and down the entire length of keys; go through all the frequencies. Then pick out a few, one at a time, up and down and all over the place.

- Make a noise!

- Explore until you begin to find a range of notes that appeal to you, ones that you want to sing.

- Now play them one at a time, continuing your yawning and stretching as though quite careless about the whole thing, as noisily as you like. While you are yawning in this way, keep playing the notes and let your voice 'fall in' with each note you play, as if by accident: E-I-E-I-O.

- Repeat.

A CHOICE OF FREQUENCIES

It is important to remember that the keyboard represents a specific selection of frequencies or points of pitch – in other words, less than all the frequencies available. In this sense, the piano 'chooses' certain frequencies from the total sound range available, just as different languages could be said to 'choose' different sound patterns from our whole potential vocal sound. The English language 'chooses' certain sounds, and the Chinese language selects others; human beings can learn both speech patterns, thus enlarging their range of vocal sound. In a similar way, the keyboard does not contain the quarter-tones, or tones which are available to the player of stringed instruments, and with which Eastern and Oriental singers are familiar.

The human voice potentially contains all these frequencies, both those of our native musical culture and those of other musical cultures. We have our own 'inner keyboard' from which we can find each pitch of sound selected by the piano. This is complex; but remember, we human beings made the piano, not the other way round . . . think about it.

The inner and outer keyboard

You have begun to discover how you can move the VOB from high to low, to resonate from one part of your chest/throat/head to another.

- Imagine your own 'inner keyboard' as you did in the 'Humming up and down the back' exercise in Part Two (page 52).

- As you play from one end of the piano to the other, relate the sounds you make to the 'inner' keyboard of your voice, and allow the VOB to change from one field of resonance to another in your search for sound. Use your body. Move your back.

Remember:

1 Muscles, Mobility and Openness (MMO).

2 Vibrating Out-Breath (VOB).

3 Primitive Vocal Energy (PVE).

The sounds you find at one end of the keyboard will not 'feel' the same to you as the ones at the other. You have to adjust; you have to move muscles, open spaces. Move the VOB from one field of resonance to another, from your head to your chest. Remember: MMO, especially MOBILITY. If you can't 'find' your own voice at first, imagine it is the cat that is singing. Miaow your way along. M-N-EE-AA-OOO! Or bark. Or hoot. Search, complain, grumble, enjoy. No judgement. No beauty competitions. Play a note and then sing it: LA-LA-LA.

When you can't sing up – sing down

When a note catches in your throat, or you feel tightening or pressure, then return to the previous note, and the one before that. When you can't go up, go down. Accept your limitations as they are today. When your voice 'gives out' on the downward journey, go up – step by step, key by key, listening to the quality of each note on the keyboard as it is reflected in your voice, visiting one by one the different frequencies. Up two, down three, up four, down five and so on. Try playing and singing along using only the smaller black keys.

The black keys

The black keys have special names and a special function in relation to the white keys, which we will come to later. Right now, just play all or any of the black keys, in any order. You may notice that there is something 'tuneful' about your excursions. This is because the black notes represent the five-note or pentatonic scale and are all 'in harmony' with each other. When you play a random sequence of black and white notes you may notice strong disharmonies. When you play just the little black keys, they harmonise. Experience the differences. Vocalise on one note and then search for another note: you will create a dissonance, or disharmony.

Feeling the difference between one note and another

At this stage, you might be surprised by the totally different quality that emerges in your voice from note to note. You may even have different feelings. One note may suddenly touch you, like striking an inner chord, or arousing hidden feelings. Certain frequencies find an immediate echo, while others are difficult to feel. Play a note and listen silently. Feel the vibrations from the note you have played, without giving voice to it. Pause. Repeat. Move away from the piano. Stretch and move. Give voice on any pitch, with any sound. Listen to the vibrations of the sound you make. Try and locate the same pitch along the keyboard. Call out that particular pitch of sound: cajole it, seek it, play with it. Search while singing. Play. Improvise. You can't go wrong.

HEARING A PLEASING SOUND

Probably, while working and playing on these exercises, you will suddenly hear something pleasing in your voice: you will have become absorbed, and therefore relaxed, and the muscular mechanisms will all be functioning without the stress of too many commands or hesitations from your brain. A sound you like will emerge; and remember, at this stage, if it's pleasing to you, that's all that matters. From one sound that you feel good with, improvise a short melody with sounds or words, always ending on the note you started with. Never mind the quality – feel the sound!

> *'I'm exploring, I'm exploring, don't know where I'm going,*
> *Just up and down and round and round, having fun.*
> *I am the walrus, GOO GOO GOO JOOB.'*

Based on Lennon/McCartney, 'I Am the Walrus', 1967

HOLDING A TONE

'Holding' really means the basic action of 'sustaining'. The term 'holding' could be a bit misleading, because it might give you the idea of stopping something – like holding your breath instead of going along with the flow of it. 'Sustaining' is a better word to work with, and should remind you to widen your lower ribs. Also, you will discover, it is one thing the piano cannot do as well as you!

Sustain, carry, support, go along with; these are all descriptions that will help you understand what is required of you. You will immediately understand that you have to prepare your body to open up for the in-breath, and support the VOB: widen your lower ribs, lengthen the back of your neck, become aware of the roof of your mouth and be alert in your body position, whether standing or sitting down.

Basic training at the piano for 'singing in tune' (5–10 minutes)

- Trust your ear/voice connection to pick up and reproduce the note you play: try one in the middle range of the piano to begin with.

- Don't hesitate. Breathe in as you play the note, then let out a VOB while you can still hear the vibrations of the note played.

- Sing softly to begin with on NAAAH, NYOU, HAAAA or YEAH. You don't need to sing loudly.

- Remember that breath is the 'food' of sound: give as much attention to your in-breath as to the sound. Accept your own abilities as they are at the moment. Use your eyes as though you were aiming your sound to touch a particular spot on the wall furthest from you. You needn't set a chronometer! Just be aware of the length of your out-breath and the feeling of sustaining an even pitch.

- Play the same note again while you are singing: listen to yourself and to the vibrations of the note you have played.

As you sustain the note, you will become aware of an inward movement in the abdomen. Remember: the diaphragm contracts inwards and upwards to expel air. To slow down the contraction and sustain a sound you must use your ribs to resist and slow down the inwards/upwards contraction. Sustaining a sound is muscular work! Accept what you can do now.

Once you feel you can sustain one note on FAAYAAH or HAANNAH, develop the sound into NAAAOOOEEEE, or begin to invent little phrases that you will sing out all on the same note. 'Here I am' or 'The water is wide' or 'If I ruled the world' or 'Time for tea'. Sing on a different note and with different messages. This trains your ear to sustain a pitch while words change the shape of the sound (this idea is developed further in the next section).

Here is one student's account of a tone-by-tone journey up to the higher parts of her voice:

'This way of singing, that I wasn't at all familiar with, was there inside myself for me to pick up . . . the more I let go, the more was possible. So when I reached the higher notes, my body instinctively knew what technique to use and where I needed to open up. My body also knew that it had to keep the energy to keep the note. I held out one tone over and over again and every time I thought: 'Was that me? Can I do it again?' I started to feel a bit insecure, but I realised that if I believed the note would come, it would come. At last I 'played' with my voice, and suddenly had a natural impulse to start actually jumping up and down, and was able to reach even higher. I had known for a long time, I think, that those notes were there inside me and I felt very happy hearing them out loud.'

Try once again to experience that special co-operation between mind and body to sustain a sound when you open up and 'keep the energy'. Remember – breath is the 'food' of sound. Give as much importance to the in-breath as to the sound.

By now your first twenty minutes of singing at the piano should be up!

You can repeat and learn from the previous exercises as often as you like, before moving onto the next sequence, which has to do with 'facing' some of the basic requirements of musical structure. Any one of the exploratory exercises below can be practised on their own for another full twenty-minute session, or you can go through all of them in sequence. It's up to you to devise the combination that best suits your needs and repeat it as often as possible.

Facing the Music 1

Singing involves gaining confidence in music as much as gaining confidence in, and through, your voice. Sooner or later, to develop, we have to 'face the music' and learn some of the basics. Make a start in this section.

MUSICAL NOTIONS AND NOTATIONS

Musical notation is a huge subject that I do not propose to cover here. No, not even a single dotted crochet, breve or semibreve. But have no fear, they will find you soon enough, or you will find them. Your developing voice will lead you to them. Then you will realise that there are plenty of interesting learning resources around to help you, in both book and CD form. However, there are a few musical notions that the piano itself can help you to understand, and which will help your voice develop, and it would be churlish of me, an old piano-phobe, not to share them with you.

 **Octaves, intervals and scales**

The basic eight-note musical scale starts and ends on the same note. This is how music tries to fool us! How can something linear, like a piano, we ask, allow us to begin and end on the same note? If you can remember, from what was said about harmonics, that overtones reflect the fundamental (the note you sing or play), then things begin to fall into place. An overtone can be the same note further up, or further along – or somewhere in direct relation to the fundamental. This is reflected in the structure of the piano. As you may have noticed, the same pattern of black and white keys repeats itself over and over again. You always get the same regular arrangement of black and white keys, whichever piano or keyboard you use. A group of two black keys, then another group of three, always exactly in the same relation to the white keys.

 **Recognising and playing an octave
(As long as you need)**

The universally recognised names for the white keys are: A, B, C, D, E, F, G – in that order. There is no X, Y, Z – no, not even at the very top or bottom. The group A, B, C, D, E, F, G just repeats itself over and over again from one end of the keyboard to the other – on the white keys only. Once you know where to start a sequence, you will be able to locate every C or F or G on the keyboard straight away.

- When you sit opposite the very middle of the keyboard you will see in front of you a group of two black keys.

- Play the white key immediately to the left of the left-hand black key of this pair. This note is called Middle C. Usually it is an easy pitch for you to find and sing from in your own voice.

- Play it and give voice lightly – VOB.

- Every single time you see a white key to the left of the group of two black keys, it is called C. It occurs eight times on the full seven-octave keyboard.

- Now you know that the sequence of notes between each C represents an octave. Play any C and then all the notes, black and white along to the next C, either up or down (to right or left): an octave.

- Follow lightly with your voice. Sing the first and then the last note of the sequence. The last note is actually the first note of the next octave – and so it goes on.

Every C on the piano represents a harmonic of all the others. The lowest C is a very low rumble indeed, and the highest C almost no more than a barely audible chink. If you could play them all at the same time you would notice that they seem to agree – they harmonise.

As we have learned, the names of the keys are always in the same order: A, B, C, D, E, F, G. Once you have found C, you can now find and name the other keys, moving up the white notes of the piano.

Now find and sing an octave from B below the C or the A. Slide your voice lightly along through all the black and white in-between notes up to the following note of the same name.

HARMONISING FREQUENCIES

An octave note represents a frequency that is exactly double that of the fundamental. That's why when you play the first C and then the next one along, they sound similar but different in pitch. Middle C has a frequency of 256hz.

The next C up has exactly double the number: 512hz, and so on, beyond the reach of the piano keys and into the 'music of the spheres'.

Every octave contains many other harmonising frequencies, such as a 'third' (the first and third notes in the scale) and a 'fifth' (the first and fifth notes in the scale) – with much practice they can be clearly accentuated in overtone singing. The distance between any two tones of the scale is known as an 'interval'. Thirds, fifths and octaves are all known as 'concordant' intervals because they 'harmonise' or sound 'right' together.

RECOGNISING AN INTERVAL

'I'm singin' in the rain . . .
I'm happy again.'

Arthur Freed, 'Singin' in the Rain', 1929

An interval is what actually creates music. A melody could be described as a succession of different intervals. The piano helps you to find and recognise intervals. They are sometimes described as steps – this might be a helpful way to think about them for a while. The interval of one octave is more like a 'leap'; it is often heard in songs worth the challenge of learning to sing. The interval between two adjacent tones, or notes, is called a 'second'; from any tone to the next but one is the interval of a 'third', and so on, right up to the octave.

Some-where!

The song 'Singin' in the Rain' begins with an octave leap – that is, an interval of one octave. 'Somewhere Over the Rainbow', from *The Wizard of Oz* (1939), also begins with an octave leap.

- Play Middle C and then the next C above it, and hear the interval. If you know the melody sing it: 'Some – where!'.

- As you know, singers are not supposed to 'swoop' from the lower note to the higher one. But do a bit of 'swooping' to loosen up your voice.

- Now do a good clean 'vocal leap' from the bottom note to the top one: 'Some / where!'

It can help to think of the higher note as actually being in a similar space to the lower note – like inside your mouth (expanded buccal cavity) for instance, not way above your head! Once you know the first interval of any song – the 'step' or 'leap' required – you will be more confident about your start.

BEING READY

A musical 'interval' is also how two different notes sound in relation to each other. When somebody has a birthday, and someone in the family starts singing 'Ha. . .', the rest of us come in exactly on '. . .ppy birthday to you!' It is because we know the interval, we know and recognise the relationship between the first two notes of 'Ha-ppy' which are the same, and we 'hear' the change of note on 'birth. . .' in our minds even before it has been sung.

See if you can find the interval that begins 'Happy Birthday to You' at the piano. Sing it first, then search for the notes. Experiment. It does not matter at all which note you start on. What matters is finding the interval – the specific 'step' from one note to the next that *creates* the melody. You can try the same thing with any song you are familiar with.

MUSICAL SCALE

A musical scale is a series of full notes (or tones) and half-notes (or semitones).

A semitone is the distance between a key and the next nearest key of any colour – up or down. If you play and sing every key on the keyboard consecutively, one after the other, you will hear a succession of semi-tones. Play them and sing them very slowly, appreciating the subtle change of pitch.

In and out of the mood

Remember that tones 'move' from the previous one towards the next one. A musical scale selects a succession of tones that move in and out of each other's field of resonance to create a particular mood. The eight-tone scale in C major has a specific 'mood', which is called 'major'. It is the easiest one to find on the keyboard – because you only need the white keys. Many songs are composed using this scale of notes because of its specific 'up' mood. There are many different types of scales, and each has a specific feeling or mood. Indian ragas are a form of scale with different laws of harmony from those in Western scales. The interval pattern for the scale in C major is:

Tone – tone – tone – semitone – tone – tone – tone – semitone.

Play slowly, one by one, the eight consecutive white notes from the Middle C to the next C along. Listen to the movement of vibrations from one tone to the next. Do you get a satisfying feeling that you have completed something? That you started and you ended?

You can sing this scale, as in the song from *The Sound of Music* (1959), to: Doh, re, mi, fa, so, la, ti, doh.

'Doh' indicates the first and the last note of the octave, which can be started on any pitch.

Sing word by word the complete sequence from low to high then 'down' again.

Doh (C above)

         ti

       la

     so

   fa

  mi

 re

Doh (Middle C)

To learn the 'melody', or pitch pattern, start from the Middle C at the piano and go up note by note to the C above it and then down again.

It takes some effort to sing the sequence in reverse – we are not used to reading backwards – but once you've got it, it will stay with you.

SPIRALS

From now on, it could be far more useful to think of octaves not as linear, represented by a line of piano keys, but as spiral. Each octave comes from the previous one and goes on to the next one in a continuous spiral, upwards or downwards, and you can pick them up at any point in the spiral.

This is closer to the natural movement from high, middle to low, or low, middle to high in our voices.

Once your ear is attuned to the mood and melody of a major scale, such as C major, you will be able to find it and sing it from any starting note on the piano. You can start singing your major scale from any note and finish it on the same note one octave up or down (without having to know or play the key-pattern variation).

Walk up and slide down

Five notes up, and five notes down is a musical 'fifth'. When you have learned the pitch pattern, you can start on any note of the piano, in the same way as the octave.

Begin by lightly 'walking' your voice, step by step, from Middle C. Then 'slide' your voice down, ignoring the steps.

```
                          so    so
                                fa
                    fa
                                   mi
              mi                     re
                                       Doh
        re
   Doh
```

Once you have learned to sing this pitch pattern up and down, you can play with it vocally. Move around as you sing; move your back and mime the movement of sliding with your arms to accompany the movement in your voice. Five notes: one, two, three, four, five.

Dramatise the sound, play with the sound, laugh through the sequence:

HA-HA-HA-HA-HA!

Then slide or glide down through each pitch:

OOOOOOOOooooooo!

Use your body: move away from the piano, coming back to check your pitch every so often.

By now, another twenty-minute session at the piano will be up. Time to relax and reflect.

SHARPS AND FLATS

Nothing can be more unsettling to the confidence of a new singer than to be told, usually with a certain disparagement: 'That was a bit flat, wasn't it?' Or: 'Didn't you think you were a bit sharp on that note?' What do they mean? Basically they mean that according to them you were not singing 'in tune'. If you were 'sharp', you were singing slightly off and *above* the note, and if you were considered to be 'flat', you were singing slightly off and *below* the note in question. Musicians actually write in sharps and flats to indicate when they want this effect, and it's considered good to do it when required, but not otherwise.

Singing 'on the note' is largely a question of energy and alertness. Singing flat (below the note played) is usually an indication of low energy, often linked to a lack of confidence in the voice. Singing sharp (above the note played), on the other hand, usually indicates too much uncontrolled energy, and a certain panic about getting things 'right'. As you gain confidence in your singing body, and learn how to move your vocal energy more freely, you will gradually have fewer and fewer problems with singing either 'sharp' or 'flat'.

THE DROSS

The piano, or any instrument, can be a good music teacher, but it can also be a hard taskmaster for the voice, presenting us with what could be called 'pure sound', in comparison with which, especially if you are searching for the perfect instrumental sound, you may well hear your own voice as 'imperfect' or even 'flawed'.

> *'I must lie down in the place where all the ladders start,*
> *In the foul rag-and-bone shop of the heart.'*

W.B. Yeats, 'The Circus Animals' Defection', 1938

Try thinking of the 'less than perfect' sounds that emerge as belonging to the 'rag and bone shop of the voice'! As you practise at the piano, think of it as another form of 'ladder', helping you climb up and down into your own voice. When you listen to these 'imperfect' vocal sounds, give them time and take them seriously, rather than rejecting them; they may become rather the opposite – full of life and strength. During the process of transformation they can often lead you towards your own miraculous voices, turning, in an alchemical way, from dross into gold.

Shaping the Sounds of Speech

Words create another form of music: language teaches us a tune, shaping the sound of our voices as well as organising our thoughts. Like music, words provide another framework and structure within which the voice can develop. Words, and the rhythms of language, inspire melodies. When the words are alive and cherished, the song wakes up: it becomes full of pith and energy. When we don't give words their full dynamic value, the rhythms of song are dulled. We need to reacquaint ourselves, through bodily awareness and imitation, with our 'golden age', when our tongues first tasted the pleasure of a new word or phrase. Active listening is an important part of this re-learning process. By learning and loving again the music of words, our singing will increase in depth and meaning.

ARTICULATION AND THE UNSTRUNG TONGUE

An 'unstrung tongue' is a flexible tongue: one that is able to get around all sorts of verbal sounds with enjoyment and relish. It signifies the ability to articulate clearly. A virtuoso of the 'unstrung tongue' was the actor-comedian Danny Kaye. He was also a brilliant musical entertainer, who used a full vocal range, from bass to soprano, with total flexibility and verbal clarity. Listen to him singing 'Manic Depressive Pictures Presents: Lobby Number' from the film *Up in Arms* (1944) or watch him perform 'Symphony for Unstrung Tongue' in the film *The Secret Life of Walter Mitty* (1947).

'Elocution . . . a word that stretches the lips as it raises the hackles.'
Paul Fisher, *Daily Telegraph*, 24 March 2001

This section is really about diction, or elocution. But I don't like either word: they contain far too many associations of 'right' and 'wrong', 'good' and 'bad', and not nearly enough of the pleasure principle. As the French actor Jean-Louis Barrault once said, 'Speech and expression are not two separate things: they are not apple and pear, but altogether peach!' Diction, when it is separated from expression, is likely to produce neither peaches nor plums but only dried-out prunes. So let's not think of 'diction', let's look for the music of words, so that we can set them dancing in song.

'The song depends before all else on the words.'
Umm Kulthum, Egyptian singer

FORM AND CONTENT

A word spoken aloud or sung has, like a peach, both form and content in its sound structure. The peach contains juicy flesh, given shape or form by a soft yet firm outer skin. Consonants are like that: the outer skin around the vowels, or the flesh, of each word. Alternatively, you could think of consonants as the paper round the chocolate, or as the frame around the painting, or the walls and doors of a room. They give definition. The vowels are what is inside: the juice, the taste, the substance, the space, the imagination, the breath. The sound pattern of each spoken word is created by both vowels and consonants – take away either one and the world of words collapses. We form words by moving and changing the volume and shape of the inside of our mouth and throat. We learn to sculpt words with our tongue, lips and throat, and at the same time the words themselves slowly sculpt the shape of our lips and mouths. YES, YES, makes for a different shape of mouth than OH, OUI, OUI, OUI!

Looking at vowels

'Climb ev'ry mountain, ford every stream,
Follow ev'ry rainbow, till you find your dream.'

Oscar Hammerstein II, 'Climb Ev'ry Mountain',
from *The Sound of Music*, 1959

Do you climb every 'mountayne'? Or 'mountin'? Or 'mounten'? How do you voice that 'a i n' sound? And if you decide to climb every 'mounten', then are you going to follow every 'renbow'? Where are the rules? Confusing, isn't it?

Clearly comprehensible pronunciation is what communicates clearly to your listener. This can vary according to the influences of family and environment, and of what is considered 'normal'. But no matter which cultural or environmental influences guide your pronunciation of a word, giving you the sound and accent that are a part of your personality, one thing remains constant. When you sing it is *always* the vowels in the word (plus specific consonants) that connect with your breath and carry the tone of your voice. In order to explore this phenomenon, rather than give you an exhaustive list of every vowel and vowel combination in the English language, I suggest we work with what are known as the 'root vowels', in a traditional way. When you can make the connection with breath and resonance through the five root vowels (plus one), you will be able to adapt all your speech to this principle, keeping normal vowel sounds intact with whichever pronunciation is most authentic or appropriate for you.

Remember: Muscles, Mobility and Openness (MMO), Vibrating Out-Breath (VOB), Primitive Vocal Energy (PVE) – and now something new:

- A. E. I. O. U.

These sounds are known as the 'root vowels' and are better used with Italian pronunciation, in order to connect them to the breath and make more space for them inside the mouth, and thus more resonant sounds. One more vowel sound is needed to keep the connection with the English language (where it occurs a lot) and with PVE: UH – pronounce it as in PUP.

- AA. EH. EE. O. OO. UH.

The Root Vowels . . . and Uh

Each vowel sound (and every other spoken word) causes our muscles to shape the air passageway differently for our outgoing breath. Our muscles work together, contracting or extending to make the inner space either smaller or larger, and directing the VOB towards different parts of the hard palate.

- Whisper aloud each vowel sound softly, one after the other as you read. Feel the involvement of the vocal folds. Notice how each vowel opens the space inside your mouth differently, and observe the effect on the VOB and resonance.

  AAAH as in FAR or SCARF.

  E – EH as in FAIR, or RARE or AIR.

  I – EE as in GREEN or FREEZE.

  O – O as in *Jonathon Jo has a mouth like an O*; make it as full as you can.

  U – OO as in *COOEE!* or YOU.

  UH – UH as in LOVE or YOUNG.

Did you feel a movement at the level of the vocal folds? This is quite normal when you whisper. The folds often 'speak' the vowels before the lips.

- Speak aloud or sing each of the six vowel sounds, one after the other, following the pronunciation guide:

  AA. EH. EE. O. OO. UH.

- Repeat each sound as often as you need until you feel the full difference between them. Speak them short and speak them long.

- There are nineteen separate muscles in the human tongue. It is very mobile. Observe how active, or how relaxed, your tongue becomes when you speak or sing.

- Recite the following, keeping your tongue as relaxed as you can:

  Every spoken or sung vowel makes a different shape inside my mouth, and affects the quality of resonance.

Three ways to give six vowels a work-out

These explorations are similar to the one suggested for resonance in Part 2 (page 95). The aim is to give you a real feeling of how you 'reshape' the inside of your mouth – how you can redirect the VOB to different parts of your hard palate, or roof of your mouth, using your tongue, cheeks and lips.

Practise the following exercises with each of the six vowels:
AA. EH. EE. O. OO. UH.

Finding more space for vowels inside the mouth

* Speak aloud and 'place' the vowel in the front of your mouth, close to your upper teeth and lips.

* Place the vowel further back into the middle of your mouth, under the hard palate.

* Place the vowel at the back of the throat.

* Observe the difference in feeling and pitch. Try and feel where the highest point of resonance is for each vowel – whether it is towards the middle, back or front of your mouth.

Singing the six main vowels at the keyboard

* Sing the six main vowels one by one at the piano. Sing them one at a time, on a single note. Sing all six on one note, one after the other without a break. Continue to give as much attention to your in-breath as to your VOB.

* Observe the change in the feeling of each vowel as the pitch changes. Sing five vowels up and down a fifth and then all six up and down six consecutive pitches.

Discovering qualities of expression

* Discover just how expressive a single vowel sound can be.

* Express different feelings or attitudes using one vowel at a time.

* Then through all six vowels:

Questioning:	A?	EH?	EE?	O?	OO?	UH?
Commanding:	AA.	EH.	EE.	O.	OO.	UH.
Mocking:	AA.	EH.	EE.	O.	OO.	UH.
Joyful:	AA!	EH!	EE!	O!	OO!	UH!
Doubtful:	AA.	EH.	EE.	O.	OO.	UH.
Seductive:	AA.	EH.	EE.	O.	OO.	UH.
Fearful:	AA!	EH!	EE!	O!	OO!	UH!
Happy:	AA.	EH.	EE.	O.	OO.	UH.

* Continue with as many different emotions as you can think of.

- Raise and lower the pitch and volume as you wish: be dramatic and expressive, ask questions, make comments. Observe how and whether your facial expression changes. Remember your in-breath.

Vowels are created in the vocal folds, as well as being shaped in the whole space from the larynx to the lips, including the roof of the mouth and the space behind the nose.

The six root vowels can be worked together with the 'Hourglass' exercise as described on page 108.

Open-mouthed vowels

- Speak or sing the following phrase, making as much space as possible within the mouth for each vowel, remembering MMO on the in-breath. Breathe as often as you want to.

  'If I ruled the world, every day would be the first day of Spring' (Leslie Bricusse, 'If I Ruled the World', from *Pickwick*, 1963).

- Repeat, moving the whole body. Dance. Exaggerate! Bring the phrase to life!

Because vowels play such an important role in carrying breath and tone (VOB) we need to find their full value in each spoken or sung word. The tendency in normal speech is to squash or flatten them. In singing it is particularly important that we find a way to sustain them and give them their full value.

The tongue is known as 'the dancer' in Indian singing.

Nasalisation

Squashing, flattening, or 'nasalisation' of vowels often results more from a tight lower jaw or a tense tongue than from chronic sinus trouble. Nasalisation is a way of holding back your voice, and is linked to a lack of confidence. As you practise these exercises your confidence will grow, and nasalisation will only be there when you want it. The following exercise is intended to exaggerate some of the movements that can produce nasalisation, so that you can more clearly recognise the sound:

- Speak aloud or sing the following phrase, keeping your jaw tight and pulling the front of your tongue backwards into the middle/back space of your mouth, with your jaw immobile.

  'If I ru̲led th̲e wo̲rld, e̲very da̲y wo̲uld be̲ th̲e fi̲rst da̲y o̲f Spri̲ng.'

- Notice the increase in nasalisation?

- Now do the opposite: Yawn your way through with a fat lazy tongue in the bottom of your mouth.

  '(Yawn) I̲f I ru̲led (yawn) th̲e wo̲rld, (yawn) e̲very da̲y (yawn) wo̲uld be̲ th̲e (yawn) fi̲rst da̲y o̲f Spri̲ng.'

- Observe the difference in the sound of your voice. There are many opportunities to 'yawn' open more space for vowels thus making more room for your voice to resonate fully.

- Yawn your way through the following list. Stop the consonants from squashing the vowel!

  RIGHT – yawn – AROUND – yawn – GLAD – yawn – FINE – yawn HAND – yawn – ELEPHANT – yawn – TAN – yawn – DRUNK – yawn – APPLE – yawn – LUCKY

  SUNSHINE – yawn – FUN – yawn – ROUGH – yawn – TOUGH – yawn – LOVE – yawn – CHUM – yawn – FLOWER – yawn – SUMMER – yawn – BROTHER . . . smile . . .

'THE MAGIC OF YOUR SMILE'

As far as the spoken word goes, the 'magic of your smile' really depends on how much you are able to open out that little 'i' vowel hiding inside and stop it being pushed up into the back of the nose. Stretch your smile – not just from ear to ear, but by releasing your tongue and jaw:

SM-AH-ILE!

Voicing short vowels

There are some vowels that really challenge you to sing them. It's easy to say 'give me a kiss', but quite another thing to sing those three short vowels! First, define the vowel sound. Sing it. Connect it to your breath. Feel where the VOB goes in your mouth. Watch your tongue movement. Are you doing too much? Sing/slide the vowel sound from different notes at the piano. Let VOB rise. Experiment to find the sound you want. Then sing the whole word, allowing space for the vowel. Try with the following groups of words – sing them high, sing them low:

WISH. FISH. KISS.

WINK. THINK. PINK.

NEW. FEW. CUE.

CREED. BLEED. PLEAD.

WEIGHT. FATE. PLAYED.

WORD. BIRD. PURRED.

LURE. CURE. VIEW.

TEA. ME. HE. MEAN.

Voicing compound vowels

In the following list of words there are combinations of at least two different vowel shapes. Explore them. Decide how to open them out and give them more space, either through the root vowels or in other ways that keep the normal vowel sound intact. Enjoy them!

FIRE. HOW. PROUD. FROWN. VIEW. JOY. SHY. LURE. FRY. BOWER.

A MULTI-VARIABLE APERTURE

Seen in a purely mechanistic way, the space from the larynx to the lips could be seen as a 'Multi-Variable Aperture' – let's call it 'MVA'. The aperture through which we blow air through wind instruments is in a fixed shape. Humans are capable of making an infinite variety of different shapes through which to blow the air of our 'trumpets'.

Shaping the aperture

> *'Time is so old, and love so brief,*
> *Love is pure gold; and time a thief.'*

Ogden Nash, 'Speak Low', from *One Touch of Venus*, 1943

Take a phrase from a song, one syllable at a time. Whisper through the phrase, shaping the 'aperture' for each sound and feeling the changes in shape between larynx and lips. Feel how the word or syllable defines the shape inside your mouth (the aperture) for the VOB to pass through the mouth or up behind the roof of the mouth and out through the nose. When you have 'rehearsed' and fully felt the shape of each syllable, repeat the exercise, singing lightly on each word. Then repeat with more confidence, sustaining each vowel and giving value to all the consonants.

Trumpet solo

Using the root vowels and the consonants T, D, R, P and B, play with the idea of 'trumpeting' sound.

Give yourself time to experience the change in your MVA. Play with the sounds and mime the trumpet in your hands!

PA-PA-PA-PA-PA!

TA-RA-TA-RA-TA!

BEH-BEH-BEH-BEH!

DEE-RI-DI-DEE-DEE!

DOH-DOH-DOH-DOH!

TOO-TOO-ROO-TOOT-TOOT!

GOO-GOO-GOO-JOO!

The taste of consonants

Consonants are truly delicious. DELICIOUS. DEE-LISCHIOUSSSSSS! Feel them on the tip of your tongue and between your lips: MMMMMMM! Play with them, taste them, savour them. DDDDDDDD, then TTTTTTT, then again BBBBBBB, or even PPPPPP. How about RRRRRRR? What an extraordinary sound that is. Think how many of the nineteen little muscles in the tongue are being exercised by that one sound: RRRRRRRRR. What about G, and K – and ZZZZ, and FFFFF? What about combinations of consonants: GRRR, or MRRR, or TZ-TZ, CHK, CHK, KCHK, SKTT SKTT, or even TFS, TFS, or SVT,

SVT? When was the last time you explored the different possibilities of all the consonants in the alphabet? Every once in a while we should give it a try if only to appreciate the incredible flexibility of our tongue and lips.

Un-singable sounds

B, CH, D, G, K, P and T are called 'plosive' consonants. They actually stop the out-going passage of air for a split second. Read aloud the list, and try to feel what happens: B, CH, D, G, K, P, T.

Exaggerate. Observe both the similarities and differences in the way your tongue and lips move to form these consonants and stop the outgoing air. It is impossible to sing them. Then discover what they do when they precede a vowel. Try speaking them out loud in connection with the five root vowels. Then find any song text to read through for the pleasure of sounding consonants and appreciating the value of vowels.

> 'Tell me he's lazy, tell me he's slow;
> Tell me I'm crazy (maybe I know).'

Oscar Hammerstein II, 'Can't Help Lovin' Dat Man',
from *Showboat*, 1927

The singing consonants

Notice other consonants, such as L, M, N and NG. Feel how they are 'voiced' by the movement of your tongue directing the VOB through the back of your nose, as you do when you hum. They are the 'singing consonants'. By letting these consonants 'sing', you can introduce a specific 'blues' or gospel quality and feeling into your song.

> 'Oh your daddy's rich, and your ma is good lookin'.'

Ira Gershwin, 'Summertime', from *Porgy and Bess*, 1935

In her interpretation of 'Summertime', the jazz singer Sarah Vaughan lingers on the final 'N' until it positively vibrates: 'Oh your daddy's rich, and your ma is good *lookinnnnnnnn*.' It adds to the hot and lazy feeling she has already established. Singing consonants serve the same purpose as vowels – that of opening up the emotional content of the song.

Another well-known jazz singer, Cab Calloway, draws out the singing consonant 'L' in the song 'Who Calls' with great effect, emphasising his longing for the caller:

> 'Who ca<u>ll</u>s? When a star fa<u>ll</u>s from above,
> Can it be the one I <u>lo</u>ve? Who ca<u>ll</u>s?'

Cab Calloway, 'Who Calls?', 1941

Playing with consonants

You can experiment with both the 'plosive' and the 'singing' qualities of consonants, and you can use certain consonants to give extra 'bite' to words. You can use them for their percussive effects in certain kinds of jazz singing, and, to give dramatic emphasis, you can stress them – and you can also learn to soften them when you need to, using the tip of your tongue lightly. Your words can be made to snarl or to purr, to bite or to caress, depending on how you combine vowels and consonants. Try snarling or purring the following phrase:

> *'I don't stay out late, don't care to go,*
> *I'm home about eight, just me and my radio.'*

> Fats Waller, 'Ain't Misbehavin'', 1945

From consonants to vowels

- Change the emphasis from consonants to vowels on the following words and see how the feeling changes.

  LOVE. COME. SIT. FOLLOW. LIFE. PITY. LONG. LOOSE. GOLDEN. FEAR. HAIR. BIRD. TEETH. WARM. FIRST.

- First stress the consonants – and then give more breath to the vowels.

- Feel the work going on in the 'Multi-Variable Aperture' (the MVA) inside the mouth.

- Try making as little movement as possible with your jaw or cheeks; concentrate on your tongue and lips.

Throwing words up in the air

The following exercise will help you feel the sound of each word as a whole. For this exercise you will need a ball. A small beach ball is best.

- Sing the following phrase, one word at a time:

  IF. I. RULED. THE. WORLD.
  EVERY. DAY. WOULD. BE. THE. FIRST. DAY. OF. SPRING.

- Throw the ball up on the first consonant, or letter, of each word.

- While the ball is in the air, sing out the vowel sound, letting the pitch move freely and keeping the vowel 'in the air' for as long as the ball is in the air.

- When you catch the ball, end the word, stressing the final consonant where there is one.

- Now throw the ball higher and higher on each word, continuing to sing out the vowel as long as the ball is in the air. Move around as you do this.

Scat-Cats

'Scat' singing has a lot to do with developing the ability to play with variable pitch and with improvised compositions of vowels and consonants. This depends a lot on being able to give the consonants their full percussive value.

- Play with the following, changing pitch as rapidly as you can, in free jazz style:

  DO-WAH, DO-WAP, DO-WAP-DAP-DO, PA-DA, CHI-CHI-BA-DA, BA-DA-BOO, DIP-UM, BUP-UM, TA-WA-TOO-TI-LIP-TOO, NA-WA-LOO, BEE-DO-BEE-DO-BEE-YEAH-BE-DO!! BEDOOP BEDEEP BADUM BOOP! DIDLIDOBEDO DAH!

- Now see how fast you can speak or sing:

  Jump down, turn around and pick a piece of cotton!

- No cheating, get your lips and tongue around every single consonant!

- Repeat, taking any of the previous phrases up and down from the top to the bottom of your vocal range and back again – squeaks, growls and all!

The vowel stream

The following exercises will help you explore how to lengthen vowels so that they run into one other, and to carry consonants along on this 'vowel stream' as you sing.

- Speak or sing the following lines, keeping a continuous flowing sound within the vowels from one word to the next:

  Row, row, row your boat,
  Gently down the stream.
  Merrily, merrily, merrily, merrily,
  Life is but a dream.

- Do you feel the vowels carrying the consonants and the melody?

- Now repeat, singing through the first two lines of the verse with the vowels only, running them together into one 'stream' of sound, on one breath only:

  O-O-O-UH-O-EH-EE-AAHOO-UH-EEE.

- With the next two lines, pick out just the consonants:

MRRLY, MRRLY, MRRLY, MRRLY, LF S BT DRM.

- It's difficult to sing the melody, but you get a lot of fun from the consonants, don't you?

- Now speak or sing through the whole verse, giving value to both vowels and consonants.

- Do the same exercise with any song, choosing different styles, and see what happens. For instance, the beautiful and romantic poem by Robert Burns: 'My love is like a red, red rose, that's newly sprung in June', loses all its romance if the consonants are stressed, but they must be there, like the firm skin around the peach. You touch the consonants lightly but firmly into life with your tongue.

MMO, VOB, MVA and the unstrung tongue

- Articulate the following list softly, or whisper it repetitively as we did in infancy, so that you really get the feel of each sound.

Da . . . Ja . . . La . . . Na . . . Ra . . . Sa . . . Ta . . . Xa . . . Za . . . Ya

- Keeping your lips open and relaxed, speak through the list, becoming aware of the movement of your tongue. Notice how much or little you need to move your jaw to articulate a consonant in this open-mouthed position.

- Sing/chant a soft open-mouthed AAH sound. Think of it as an ongoing stream of sound. Breathe whenever you need to, to sustain an easy sound. Keep including the muscles of respiration in your field of awareness. Breathe in through an open mouth whenever you need to.

- Now chant the line of consonants and include them in the AAH sound, without breaking the continuous chanting line except to breathe in.

aSaaaaaaRaaaaaaGaaaaaaMaaaaaaPaaaaaaDaaaaaNaaaaaaaSaaaaaaRaaaa GaaaaMaa

- You will gradually begin to feel as though you are sliding the consonants onto a continuously moving stream of sound, touching them lightly into life. The important thing is to learn to keep up the stream of air/sound underneath, within or through the consonants.

- Now try the same thing with the 'plosive' consonants. Keep them calm and unexplosive!

aaaaaaaaBaaaaCaaaaHaaaaDaaaaGaaaaKaaaPaaaaaaTaaaaaaa

This, and any of the previous exercises, can be practised at the piano. Sing through them at different pitches and in different parts of your voice. Play. Explore. Experiment.

> *'(A-wa a-wa) Si-bona kwenze ka kanjani*
> *(A-wa a-wa) Amanto mbazane ayeza.'*

Paul Simon, 'Diamonds on the Soles of her Shoes', 1986

WORD AND IMAGE

When we make words fully audible to ourselves, we hear and feel more intensely the image associated with each one. Words are 'signifiers' – not the thing itself. The power of words is such that given full value they can evoke a complete sense of the reality of the image. Singing brings us closer to the time when signifier and reality were one for us. For example, in infancy we used the word 'hot' entirely in the present tense in response to heat. Later we learn to use the word 'hot' in the past and future tense and to abstract it from reality. We have learned to do the same thing with words such as 'love': we have learned to separate a word from its meaning. In singing, we have to return to the original meaning of words: we have to use words and music to bring stories and feelings off the page and back into 'real' life.

> *'FEVER! In the morning,*
> *FEVER all through the night . . .*
> *FEVER – till you sizzle.*
> *What a lovely way to burn!'*

John Davenport and Eddie Cooley, 'Fever', 1956

There is nothing academic about this song – the singer who sings it has a fever – at least as long as the song lasts. The fever is 'now'. The word, given voice and rhythm, wakes up the imagination. We relive the fever, not for real, but 'as if', and with the pleasure of playing. Play with the word FEVER. Speak or sing it out loud in different ways until it makes you shiver! FEVER!

Messages and associations

* Look at the following words. Speak them one at a time, and let them speak to your imagination and gather associations and images.

FOREVER. COME. TOMORROW. GREEN. FORGIVE. WE. AWHILE. THUNDER.

- At the piano, sing each word one at a time on each note of a scale.
- Observe how your voice changes with each tone, and how the pitch of sound can, if you let it, change your feeling and what the word expresses for you.
- Listen. Let images appear and feelings come and go.
- Compose short songs with one or all of the words.
- Choose your own words, any words you like, the most ordinary words can convey the most evocative messages.

'The wild and windy night that the rain washed away,
Has left a pool of tears crying for the day.'

Lennon/McCartney,
'The Long and Winding Road', 1967

Summary of Part Three

- Vocal sound results from a combination of breath, vibration and resonance.

- It is possible for a single voice to fill an entire cathedral.

- The human body has 'power' centres for resonance which are there to be contacted and which give colour and meaning to vocal expression.

- Overtone singing is a meditative form of singing that develops the ability to accentuate all or any of the harmonics of the fundamental note sung.

- The phrase 'singing in tune' should really be 'singing in tune with someone or something'.

- A frequency refers to the rate of sound vibrations per second.

- The piano is a useful instrument because you do not have to learn to play it in order to use it to explore your voice.

- Trust your ear/voice connection to pick up and reproduce the note you play.

- The basic eight-note scale, or octave, begins and ends on a note of the same name.

- Once your ear is attuned to a melody you will be able to sing it from any starting note on the piano that best suits your voice.

- A word spoken aloud or sung has, like a peach, both form and content, the skin being the consonants, the flesh being the vowels.

- There are nineteen separate muscles in the human tongue.

- We are capable of making an infinite variety of different shapes out of the spaces between the larynx and the lips. It can be described as a 'Multi-Variable Aperture', or MVA.

- In singing, we use words and music to bring stories and feelings back to life. The story is 'now'.

Voice: Mind, Heart, Body, Sound and . . . Imagination

'Let us now crawl,' said Bernard, 'under the canopy of the currant leaves, and tell stories. Let us inhabit the underworld. Let us take possession of our secret territory.'

Virginia Woolf, *The Waves*, 1931

FOUR

Voice: Mind, Heart, Body, Sound and . . . Imagination

Freeing the Imagination

Entering the imagination is like taking possession of a secret territory, inhabiting the underworld. It is a land of the possible, which we all inhabited actively in infancy, often leaving it behind too soon, and without having really understood its purpose. To enter that territory allows you to exercise another kind of muscle, the imagination – which, like any other muscle, shrinks and atrophies if it is neglected. We can exercise our imaginative ability through vocal explorations – it will then be freely available to help you engage with the text of any song you wish to sing with empathy and imagination.

METAMORPHOSIS AND VOICE

The voice has a greater power of metamorphosis than the body – it can express a multitude of sounds that seem to have very little relationship to your actual size, shape, ethnic group, social class or age. You can sound very small or exceedingly large; you can pretend that you are twice your size and three shades lighter or darker in colour and twenty years older or younger. In the mind of the listener you may take on the most amazing shapes. Often in workshops I ask students to close their eyes as they listen to a fellow student exploring the different sounds in their voice. From just one note, listeners can 'see' an entirely different body, or be transported to quite a different place. Visualisation can allow the mind to move away from narrow technical concerns, and to perceive and tackle obstacles as 'out there', rather than in an anxious, pernickety way as within the muscular structures. This sort of visualisation activity works best in conjunction with the basic groundwork covered in Parts One to Three, as part of the total process. To link up with the imagination we have to take the focus off the voice. We have to begin to think about the voice in metaphors and images. We have to imagine it as like a fire, a flower, a bee, a torrent, a tree, a rock, a river or a place.

VOICE AS A PLACE

The following account, written after a voice exploration at the keyboard, offers you the opportunity to share in a student's experience of working with voice and image.

'I got the image of voice being not only sound and movement through space, but a 'place' in itself. The searching was like trying to establish a territory for oneself, marking the borders of one's personal space here but no further but always with the possibility of stretching the borders just a little more, expanding the place with another few pitches. This was a fascinating concept to explore, which eventually allowed me to take my voice to pitches – places – it's never been before. At first I was working with the lower pitches, where I am sort of familiar, and I wasn't sure what to actually do with the image. Voice is a place, fine…but then what? I didn't seem to get as much sound as I wished. There was something blocking. Suddenly the image of a circular space, a circular place, with me in the middle, seemed to make sense. The sound was moving like ripples of water away from me. By adding more energy to the voice, the place I claimed for my voice grew. It took the whole focus away from technique and instead helped build a sense of curiosity. Instead of focusing on, 'Is this sounding pure? Can I reach another pitch? Am I too high up?' It helped me to think, instead, 'Is there more room? What can I do in this place?' That made it easy to slide between tones and go high up in the voice, probably higher than I've been for years…it was easy.'

Voice and image
(At least 15 minutes at the keyboard)

- First: 'snake', shake, stretch, yawn, 'sgrumble', smile, sing/slide to 'get the motor going'.

- Then revise some of the work from the previous section, this time on a whisper:

  GROUND. HEART. VALLEY. HARBOUR. HILLSIDE. TREE. WAY. SHIP. WORLD.

- Next: speak each word, out loud, 'tasting' consonants and vowels. Repeat, singing lightly.

- Find and hold the 'Multi-Variable Aperture' (MVA), to give each vowel sound a clear shape.

- Add the word *'my'*, to each of the words – for instance, 'My tree'.

- Let images come into your mind, through a process of free association, always going back to singing the original word for inspiration.

- Sing each word up and down the piano, from low to middle and high in whichever order is suggested by your voice

- Begin softly, and then let your impulse guide you, but always *on the note*.

- *Follow* the sound of each sung note; let the sound of your voice *lead* – try not to plan what your voice *should* sound like.

> *'The imagination is like the connecting fluid, it is the thing that joins all the pieces up, giving them meaning, fullness and life.'*
>
> Joseph Clark, singer, director, teacher

VOICE AND THEATRE

Theatre is about imagination, theatre is about re-imagining yourself: being who you are not. Paradoxically, the process of learning a part and becoming 'someone else' then teaches you more about who you actually are. Theatre is about taking off *and* putting on masks. Similarly, through taking on imaginary shapes, forms and characters, and expressing them vocally, you discover sounds and expressions otherwise hidden from you – which are nonetheless a part of the whole voice spectrum. The imagery allows you to explore the extremes, the unknown. An image entered into, or taken on as a kind of disguise, gives you permission to use voices and show feelings that you may be inhibited about expressing in your normal everyday life.

THE POWER OF THE IMAGE

Through the imagination, the human voice can take on a thousand roles, both human and animal. All this adds to the palette of texture and colour available to you when you search for your own individual interpretation of a song – it all becomes a conscious part of your own voice.

Where is your originality? It is in the full span of your voice as you discover and develop it through the imagination.

BEING 'SOMEONE ELSE'

A student of mine said, 'But my voice is too thin; I've no ear; I don't like the sound of my voice; I can't sing well.'

'Okay, then,' I said, 'forget the person who can't sing: become someone who can. Sing as though you were at least three times your actual size, had a dozen kids, ran a butcher's shop in the back streets of Naples – and your man has just run off with the florist.' I remember clearly the look of amazement on her face, and then the look of excitement – even relief. She could change – she could actually change? Just through an image? Suddenly her voice took off, she rolled up the sleeves of her designer shirt, kicked off her shoes and got going. The picture allowed her to contact her own anger and humour safely, and her 'thin' little voice doubled and trebled as if by magic. She was singing and laughing; her whole physique, as well as her voice, had changed: her face was alive and expressive, inspired by the image.

The character I conjured up for that student was built up out of opposite characteristics to those I saw in the person in front of me. Big, when she was small; tough, when she was apparently fragile; humorous, when she was withdrawn and shy. The image was intended to take her as far away from her reality as possible. To give her a mask to help unmask her voice. The character was a sort of caricature, 'larger than life' – and that worked.

Singing opposites

This is an exercise to help you combine sound, words, pitch, facial expression, gesture and imagination.

- Study the list below, and choose a pair of opposites that appeal to you. Use different vowel sounds to sing on, and then let the image or idea influence the sound. If you want to, sing a word or a phrase inspired by the image. Each image brings along with it a different facial expression and gesture that you will need to find. Move around actively if need be. Vocalise freely. Experiment. Play. Remember: Muscles, Mobility and Openness (MMO), Primitive Vocal Energy (PVE), Multi-Variable Aperture (MVA).

  World-weary/young. Beautiful/ugly. Tall/small.

  Thin/fat. Laughing/sobbing. Fire/ice. Soft/hard. Gentle/tough.

  Nice/nasty. Proud/humble. Sun/moon. Glad/sad.

  Large/small. Friendly/frightening. Militant/dreamy.

  Light/heavy. Male/female. Beauty/beast. Fast/slow.

- Sing each pair of opposites, one after the other, note by note, at the piano, a fifth or an octave apart, giving one expression to the lower note and one to the higher. Use words or vowel sounds.

- Explore the image; develop, play.

- If you are able to work with a partner you can begin to have 'gibberish' dialogues from the images like 'Nice/nasty', where each develops a different character.

Using the exercise to develop your ability to interpret a song:

- Sing a whole phrase of a song while you are laughing, and then while you are sobbing. For example: 'The way you wear your hat; the way you sip your tea', from the Gershwin song. Sing it laughing then sobbing by turns, then militant, then dreamy and so on.

- Working with a partner, sing through a whole short song and ask your partner to give you directions to change from one character to another.

- Your partner can direct you to alternate between one pair of opposites throughout the song. For instance, Proud/humble: 'Proud' can be indicated with the right hand and appropriate gestures, 'humble' with the left hand. You follow your partner's directions as you sing. Your partner should take you by surprise. Try this with a simple song, such as 'Three Blind Mice'. Don't worry too much about keeping the tune: just allow different vocal qualities to come into play, trust your imagination and keep following your partner's directions. Your partner can add directions for loud or soft once you are 'tuned in'.

Characters in and for the Voice

It's not enough that the 'sound' of the voice is beautiful;
that doesn't even matter very much – what is needed
is dramatic expression. And there is no dramatic expression
without imagination.

MYTHS AND LEGENDS

Literature and folk culture provide us with an abundance of images that can help with exploring the voice in this way. Strong character images, especially, allow you to 'change skin', and offer the possibility of exercising the muscle of the imagination. It is good to begin collecting or noting down images that take your fancy in a very personal way – images that really appeal to you. Keep a notebook, or collect postcards. Your images, which will suggest character, atmosphere, feeling or music, may come from mythology, from paintings, or from other sources – maybe someone you've seen in a film, or in a newspaper, or remembered from childhood.

Pulling faces

Limbering up your facial muscles can bring more life to your voice and will help you to be more receptive to your imagination.

The promptings of your imagination can lead you to change your bodily position – and also, in particular, your facial expression, which in turn affects the inner spaces that influence resonance and vibrancy. It works the other way round as well – from the outside in. If we change our expression or change our body posture and attitude we also stimulate the flow of our imagination.

Finding expression (30 seconds to 3 minutes)

- Using both hands, give your face an all-over massage. Use your fingertips and thumbs, applying pressure in small circles, moving the fleshy parts over the solid bone structure. Gently pinch and pull your skin, especially over the cheekbones and eyebrows.

- Yawn and stretch every part that can move as you do so. Include the whole of your head, making the scalp move as well.

- Breathe in. Squeeze the whole of your face into one tight expression. Scrunch it all into one small point.

- Breathe out. Open the whole of your face – relaxing your jaw, opening your mouth wide, opening your eyes wide, lifting your eyebrows. Keep that expression, and breathe both in and out. Observe the change in your expression and feeling.

- Breathe in; now, on the out-breath, lower your eyebrows and turn down your mouth into a downwards expression. Again, hold the expression as before. Observe your feeling.

- Repeat as for the two first expressions, this time smiling with your mouth wide open, lifting your eyes and every part of your face upwards. Hold, breathing in and out.

- You can use these basic facial expressions to inspire you to many variations, imagining different 'masks' to hold and breathe through. Once you allow yourself to feel them, you will notice how they begin to influence your inner feeling and your breathing. The expression on your face 'suggests' new sounds to your imagination, and vice-versa.

- Finish by pressing your fingers and the palms of your hands all over your face warmly.

Dressing up the voice (15 minutes with a partner if possible)

- Sing through a simple song, for example 'Daisy, Daisy, Give Me Your Answer, Do', or 'Oh, What a Beautiful Morning'. Now sing the same song:

  As each one of the characters in Snow White and the Seven Dwarfs.

  As Winnie the Pooh, then as Piglet.

  As any of the characters from The Jungle Book (the original Kipling version).

  As a pantomine character, such as an Ugly Sister, Mother Goose or Aladdin.

The characters of the Ugly Sisters allow expression to some of our most outrageous voices, and the Dames seem to exist for the very purpose of allowing more sober citizens the chance to 'freak out' vocally! Characters from mythology may provide you with a hook on which to hang your own imagination. Try voicing the one-eyed Cyclops or the ferocious dog Cerberus.

Going to extremes – the wicked witch

'You ain't never goin' to get nothin' by acting like an angel chile,
You better change your ways and get really wild!!'

Popular blues song

Images have great power to contact hidden sources of energy in the voice, and none more so than that of the witch. The character of the Wicked Witch of the West, from *The Wizard of Oz*, is a useful image for vocal exploration – she really doesn't care what anyone thinks! Do a 'wicked witch' version of the most sentimental song you know – and see what happens to it.

'Your looks are laughable, un-photographable,
Yet you're my favourite work of art.'

Lorenz Hart, 'My Funny Valentine', from *Babes in Arms*, 1937

Let your voice take off. Don't be afraid! Perhaps you'll end up laughing, instead of crying! Remember: let VOB rise. No pushing! Make more inner space. Remember MMO & MVA.

Cackle and shriek your way through, and see what happens; maybe the song will be stronger because of the 'witch' effect! It will certainly come alive. Try this version on the song Chaplin made famous in *Modern Times*:

'Smile though your heart is aching,
Smile even though it's breaking.

John Turner and Geoffrey Parsons,
'Smile (Though Your Heart is Breaking)', 1936

Your voice is not damaged by occasionally allowing extremes of pitch and expression to sing out. On the contrary, the power of your imagination can tap and release sources of energy and power previously held back by inhibitions and inner judgements. As Eartha Kitt famously sang:

'I wanna be evil, I wanna be bad ...
And in the theater, I wanna change my seat ...
Just so I can step on everybody's feet!'

Lester Judson and Richard Taylor, 'I Want to be Evil', 1952

IMAGINATION AND SELF–EXPRESSION

Self-expression tends, after a while, to be repetitive, limited to the immediate, the familiar, and the safe.

Imagination and fantasy take us beyond ourselves – put us at risk, open up the unknown and lead us to the unexpected and unplanned.

PARODY

The biggest trap for this kind of exploration is parody or self-parody. Self-mockery prevents you from contacting authentic sources of inspiration and takes you away from your own imagination. Listen to yourself attentively, even when you're having fun!

THE SEARCH FOR HIDDEN CHARACTERS

A student describes here how she found a totally unexpected character within her voice. The experience came out of a session focusing on image-based vocal exploration. This is what she wrote after the session:

'I had watched several of my friends explore their voices, and I felt inspired by the things I saw them achieving. It made me think I had some possibilities myself. We started with me singing in a very low voice. I was asked to sing 'here I am', and then also tell the others what I was doing and who I was (what was the identity of the voice that was coming out of me), and to say the first things that got into my mind. That helped me to go into a character, a character who after a while became an Arab woman. I was asked to stick to the Arab woman and sing in an Arabian way. It felt very strange because I wasn't imitating an Arab woman, I was this particular Arab woman and the technique of how to sing it just came to me. I felt my jaws moving almost automatically to find the right tone; my voice just kept on going, it had its own life.'

'It had its own life' is a wonderful way of describing this new way of perceiving the voice. You are not directing, but you are, as it were, 'standing aside', and letting new qualities and textures, roles and characters emerge from your voice and body, prompted by imagination and memory – and MMO!

Character roles

Four characters: four different voices and four different feelings. The warrior; the young woman; the child; the wizard/witch.

Each of these characters can suggest something to you, and will bring out a different quality and colour in your voice, either with the one-note/one-vowel singing exercise or by 'giving' the character a song to sing. Each character will offer many different and changing facets – you will become aware of these when you sing them. The stereotype, or caricature, might come to the surface when you start, but when you listen without self-mockery you leave the stereotype behind.

- Work at the piano.
- Start from the middle of your voice.
- Sing one note at a time.

You can give the character a name: sing out 'Braveheart' for the warrior, or 'Desdemona' for the woman, for instance; or improvise words appropriate for character, following the promptings of your imagination. The wizards and witches can sing out: 'I'm gonna put a spell on you!' At the piano, search up and down through the range of your voice until you find a frequency that seems to agree with, and allow you to expand, your image. Only you can tell. You may find the child image in the higher range of your voice, and warrior in the deeper range or pitch, or vice-versa: it is very personal. You could note down different qualities that arise. Let the image inhabit you. As closely as possible, *become* each one in turn. Change your facial expression, body attitude and movement.

Giving the image a voice

You have to explore patiently to voice the image. When you hear a sound in your voice that excites, pleases or satisfies you, explore more: sing out with that sound confidently. Keep the body and face involved all the time, and let the character give voice. Don't be surprised by what comes out! Once you have established a character's facial expression and voice clearly, sing a simple song pertaining to the character – whatever suggests itself to your imagination at the time. See what happens to the song! Keep the character. Choose a simple song you know, and let the warrior, child, woman in love, witch or wizard do the singing for you.

> *Qualities you find in vocal improvisation, once tapped,*
> *stay alive in your memory – they never disappear.*
> *They are there to be drawn on, to add substance*
> *and feeling to a phrase or a word.*

Animal Arias

Many animals could give us a good voice lesson! Re-inventing their cries and calls, through a combination of imagination and imitation, will bring surprising results.

Animals and birds, too, are 'characters' in a sense. In the same way that the human characters have done, they can lead you to rediscover and develop different parts of your vocal range, with more fun and more ease than if you are only concerned about achieving higher or lower notes through mere physical technique. You will find that some of the sounds are surprisingly easy to make, after all – and surprisingly human!

Explore

Singing with whales and dolphins

You can do this quite happily in your own sitting room or rehearsal room, to the accompaniment of one of the many good recordings of whale and dolphin song readily available. Whales and dolphins are known to actually play with sound much as we do. To all intents and purposes, they actually

'sing' their messages to each other. This is where you can join in with them imaginatively. Your vocalising should be easy and fun, and emerge through easy rolling and twisting body warm-up exercises on the floor. As you stretch, yawn, roll and turn your body, begin to sing/slide freely through your voice from low, middle to high. Very soon you will find yourself 'joining in with the dolphins', with a feeling of communicating through your own voice. Keep moving, rolling and stretching, as though actually in the water with them, sing through the whole range of your voice, keeping your imagination in tune with what you hear. The dolphins and whales will help you warm up your voice and remind you of the sources of pleasure in sound.

> *'We do not sing about a reindeer, or like a reindeer.*
> *We become the reindeer and the reindeer does the singing.'*

Asa Simma, Lapp/Sami singer

WHAT ANIMALS CAN TEACH YOU ABOUT YOUR VOICE

Cats can teach us to enjoy open vowel sounds, as well as how to yawn and how to let sound slide from high to low. MIAAAOOOW! Dogs can teach us to project our voices over long distances – they are used to making themselves heard! Then think about the farmyard cockerel crowing in the morning: we would be proud of such a sound. He can teach us to stretch the back of the

neck, to open up the back of the throat, to let the VOB (Vibrating Out-Breath) rise through the MVA (Multi-Variable Aperture)! As for donkeys, have you ever listened to them practising octave leaps? HEE-HAW! – HEE-HAW! Don't do it on the in-breath as they do, though – breathe in before you start. Imagining the sound of a cow lowing takes the larynx down and places resonance in the belly. Sheep play amazingly well with short staccato sounds on their 'Beh-eh-eh-eh' bleating: remember to take the sound forward and not let it get stuck in the throat; let the VOB rise. All these animals, and others too – camels or elephants, for example – can, through our imaginative voicing, lead us playfully to life-affirming qualities in our own voices, as well as giving us clever little music lessons.

SINGING WITH INTENT

Remember that animals always give voice, or sing about something. They have an intention. That is why they give voice. So when we practise making animal sounds we should choose a direction, an intention – not just 'make a sound'; the result will be more alive, and more enjoyable. For this reason, it is more useful – and also more fun – to practise animal sounds with a partner, so that you can set up a dialogue, linked to specific themes such as calling or complaining, warning and greeting, challenging or courting. It's a lot of fun to have one partner courting and the other challenging, for example. Find sounds that you can hold for a long time, and turn into sustained singing sounds.

Explore

Body and voice together
(15–20 minutes; or for as long as you are enjoying yourself)

Cat. Dog. Cockerel. Donkey. Cow. Sheep.

Choose one of the animals in the above list. Try and visualise some particular movement which is typical of that animal: a cat licking its paw, a dog panting, the way a cow hangs its head, how the cockerel steps in the farmyard and arches its neck. It is important to find a body gesture that 'speaks' to you before you start vocalising. Play with movement: you'll be surprised at how easily the animal movements suggest themselves to you. Sometimes it helps to remember how the animal looks, to visualise its expression and feel the same expression in your own face.

From the list below, choose an attitude or intention. Find a physical movement or posture that describes it, and link it with the animal you've chosen: for instance, a contented cow – or a dog defending its territory.

Attitude/Intention: Welcoming. Warning. Defending territory. Calling. Enjoying life. Asking for food. Being content. Questioning.

When you have found a clear intention and a physical movement for your animal, then – and only then – experiment with sound. Your efforts may provoke a lot of laughter; so much the better for exercising all your breathing muscles and opening wide your jaw! There's no harm in laughing. Perhaps your animal could be amused too. Try a laughing donkey or sheep, for instance. If your throat hurts, stop. Breathe, relax, remember: Let VOB rise. No pushing.

Beware of caricature and easy solutions: for instance, 'woof-woof' is decidedly more human than animal! RRAAH! UUURGH-RAAHH!

This kind of exercise is in no way scientific! It is for each person to explore and find whatever has enjoyment and meaning, knowing that everything goes, provided it is done in the right spirit.

Barking and belting

The 'belting' sound often used by singers in stage musicals is close to barking. Barking is a strongly projected and sustained clear sound from the middle part of the voice, and carries a clear intention. It can be 'thrown out', almost like a cough – but without catching in the throat. A jubilant 'huRRAAAH!' sometimes gets the feeling. Try 'throwing' the sound, just on the noise Raaah! Raaah! You can find a barking sound quite easily which is very close indeed to the powerfully projected sound that operatic tenors employ and which is similar to the natural tenor qualities in women's voices. Feel the sound in your hard palate and the back of your nose, and not in your throat. Try *sustaining* a clear sound initiated by barking – for instance, with a feeling of triumph, or of calling for attention, warning, or challenging. Then, with your throat wide open, take the barking sound into a singing sound, and sustain it for as long as possible on one note – through the throat, not from it: jaw and ribs wide!

Caterwauling

The composer Rossini wrote a duet for cats ('Duetto buffo di due gatti'). You, too, could choose to sing through an entire song just on the calling sound of MIAOOW; you will be surprised by the amount of expression cats can put into your singing!

The field is open for your experiments, and for the greater vitality and resonance of your own human voice!

Whole Voice – Broken Sound

We have wild as well as tame animals in our voice. We contain voices that are truly able to ignore gender and category, yet which are both human and personal, in touch with raw energy and raw feeling. Think of the wild sounds that erupted into our awareness in the 1960s, released by Janis Joplin and others: 'Oh Lord won't you buy me . . . a Mercedes Benz . . . ' Remember the sounds that sizzled, cracked, raged and moaned through early pop and rock music? These are the kind of sounds that make jazz and blues live, and that give vitality and freedom to popular song all over the world. You will be able to think of many more examples. They are the 'broken sounds' that exist as part of the whole voice spectrum.

It is folly to try to 'make' a broken sound, mechanically or through 'technique', without linking them to clear feeling and intention. Broken sounds are a direct result of the total fusion between feeling, imagination and physical readiness. They involve not a few, but every muscle in the body. They are not made; they are lived.

THE NOISE OF TRUE EMOTION

*'They had developed a new dimension to conversation. They ended
every speech with the word 'hiro' which means; 'like I said' . . .
To 'hiro' they added the word 'houe', a cry of joy or distress, according
to whether it was sung or howled . . . at the end of every utterance
a man stepped back, so to speak, and attempted to interpret his words
to the listener, attempted to subvert the beguiling intellect with
the noise of true emotion.'*

Catherine Tekakwitha, seventeenth-century Mohawk saint,
in Leonard Cohen, *Beautiful Losers*, 1966

The key to broken sound is the link to raw emotion. We have already observed that animals are incapable of making a sound that does not have an emotional content. The barking sounds you explored in the previous exercise may already have touched on emotional energy. Animals can give us powerful images that allow us to access the raw emotional sounds that social conventions make us hide. It's a good moment to remember the observation that scientist Charles Darwin made in his 1872 book *The Expression of the Emotions in Man and Animals*. He wrote: 'When the voice is used under any strong emotion, it tends to assume, through the principle of association, a musical character.'

Singing or howling can be either an artistic expression, as in music, or self-expression. What makes the difference is the presence or absence of imagination.

Working through the animal image allows you to rediscover and experience broken sounds. These are in reality very similar to the ones we employed with such vitality in infancy, with no damage to our vocal folds! Once you have discovered these broken sounds again, and developed them, you will be able access them by choice to express and communicate raw and intense feeling related to text and music.

Explore

Broken sound
(30 to 50 minutes undisturbed, with partner if possible)

The following exercises require, for your own freedom and enjoyment, a soundproofed working or rehearsal space, preferably with a keyboard. Have a pencil and notebook handy.

Preparation and physical readiness:

- Give yourself a ten-minute warm-up, following the body and breathing work and exercises from Part Two. 'Snake', shake, stretch, roll, yawn, sing/slide from the bottom of your voice to the top and back again. Sing gently at first, and then with progressively more energy until you feel really warm throughout, and your voice feels 'free' from the throat.

> *'. . . high in the branches of my green tree there is a wild bird singing.'*
> Karle Wilson Baker, 'The Tree', 1919

Wolf. Bull. Bear. Baboon.

- Choose your animal 'character' and then give yourself the time it takes to get into its skin. Find a movement that feels real, that expresses the animal for you. Animal images can lead to big prowling, rolling, loping

163

movements; they can take you running or leaping, engaging the whole body.

- Your preparation is important. Let the movements you find influence your breath. Relax. Pause. Go over what you've done.

- Visualise, without doing anything. When you can remember clearly what you did, then repeat it. Take your time. Pause. Reflect.

- Repeat. You do not have to be driven by the images; let them lead you, and observe yourself as you act and give voice.

Teaching your animal voices to sing on the note

- Sit at the keyboard. Play any note around Middle C – above or below it. Sing it a few times.

- Return to the animal image. Move. Breathe. Give voice to the image. Pause.

- Listen to the echo of your own 'animal' voice.

- Keep the back of your neck long. Keep your ribs wide.

- Stop if you develop a tickle in your throat. Sigh. Yawn. Relax. Move. Start again.

- Play Middle C, or another note within the range of sound you made.

- Repeat the sound you just made exactly as you made it – on pitch. Pause. Listen.

You may at first find it difficult to hear what note your animal 'voice' sings on, or it may encompass many frequencies and move rapidly from high to low. Once again, the keyboard is there as an anchor. Experiment by voicing the image on the note. This way you will be able to find sounds again; they will not be lost in the experience. They will not be 'happenings'. Each time, you will notice that your body posture and your facial expression influence the kind of sound that comes out of your mouth as a result of the image you worked with. It may have led you to some surprising discoveries.

SPRINGBOARDS INTO SONG

Surprisingly enough, this kind of exploration can provide you with spring-boards into song. Try and observe when an animal-like sound can be sustained and turned into a singing sound. Some celebrated opera singers have been known to warm up their voices by giving wolf-like howls.

Let your own vocal energy be a guide. When you stop the exercise, recap mentally. Write down words to express your experience. If you are working with a partner or in a group, give each other constructive feedback. (See in Part Six: Working with Feedback, page 198.) How 'real' was the image, how 'real' was the sound? What images did the sound itself evoke? You may find this particular exploration releases a lot of endorphins. You get a 'high' from it.

Björn Merker is a scientist who has studied 'singing' gibbons, monkeys who live in tree-tops and sing with natural soprano voices. He joined in with them once, and even from the ground the experience was so energising that he needed a day or two to recover! The experience taught him that the act of singing is a vital form of physical expression, and part of being human. After such physical and vocal exercising, you need just to lie down on your back. Relax.

Once you make the discovery that all sorts of animal-like and bird-like sounds are a part of your own natural voice spectrum — or, to put it another way, that the human voice contains within it all sorts of animal sounds — your whole voice will really start to open up. This is a good moment to start listening, or to listen afresh, to flamenco or gospel songs. If classical singing inspires you, listen with a new ear to some really dramatic passages from a composer such as Verdi. The famous Verdi Requiem, for instance, contains choruses that are intended to be sung with a visceral anger. Listen for the sounds of the wild!

The four elements

The previous explorations and exercises should have helped you discover, expand and develop the full palette of vocal colours in your voice, joining voice, body, sound, and imagination. In the following exercise you can learn to find different qualities and texture of sound through the suggestions of word images, and learn to 'anchor' your imagination by singing each image on one and the same musical pitch. The images are of the four elements: earth, water, air and fire, together with wood and metal. In classical singing, the four main elements — earth, water, air and fire — have been used to define different parts of the vocal range from high (fire) to low (earth). In this exercise you will go further and explore, for example, the sound and feeling of 'earth' or 'fire' throughout your entire range, discovering which part of your own voice most clearly gives life to the image.

It is more pleasurable to sing the images of earth and water in their Latin-derived versions, i.e. terra, or tierra, and aqua or agua. The open vowels allow you more scope for expression.

Focus on and visualise each element in turn, and take time to personalise it. You might find that metal suggests many variations, ranging from lead to gold. The image of wood could give rise to trees or forests or chopped firewood. Give voice and word to each image in turn at the piano, pitch by pitch; observe how voice and image work together in this exploration.

Voicing the elements – on the note
(20 minutes at first, then 2 to 3 minutes whenever you warm up, or for as long as you like)

- In this exercise, choose one of the following words:

  TIERRA – earth
  AQUA or AGUA – water
  AIR
  FIRE
  STEEL
  MAHOGANY

- At the keyboard, play Middle C. Sing out your chosen word. Sing the same word, raising the pitch and then lowering the pitch. Observe the change in vocal quality as you search for a sound that gives the word life and expression. When you are satisfied, and the image comes to life through your voice, choose another word and repeat the exercise.

- When you have explored the expressive qualities of three of the element images, sing them one after the other on the same note. Take a breath between each word. Notice how the quality of your voice changes, while the pitch stays the same.

- Expand the image: it could come from the idea of possession – 'my earth' or 'mi tierra', or from the enjoyable sensation of water, excitement at fire, or strength from the resilience of metal. Observe what happens when you unite imagination and feeling through your voice.

- To sing out wilder sounds 'on the note' will give a firm anchor for your imagination and a structure to your explorations. Always start clearly 'on the note' and finish by coming back to the same note, however many breaths you take in between, and however long your improvisation.

Summary of Part Four

- The imagination is like the connecting fluid: it is the thing that joins all the pieces up.

- You can discover a multitude of different qualities in your voice through taking on different characters.

- Throat and facial muscles work together, and the expression on your face influences the sounds that come out of your mouth as well.

- Through working with images of animals and birds you can discover and develop hidden parts of your vocal spectrum that allow you to touch on and work creatively with feeling and emotion.

- You can sing out strong feelings on pitch.

- You can learn to sing different qualities of sound on one and the same musical pitch.

- You can unite voice and body through feeling and imagination.

Voice: Mind, Heart, Body, Sound and Imagination into Song

'You are the music, while the music lasts.'

T.S. Eliot, 'The Dry Salvages',
from *Four Quartets*, 1941

FIVE

Voice: Mind, Heart, Body, Sound and Imagination into Song

The Creative Voice

Singing is all about totally forgetting oneself, which seems an odd thing to say at this stage. Yet consider any truly creative activity: painting a picture, preparing a good meal, designing a boat, planning a festival, or whatever; the action takes you out of yourself, makes you 'forget' yourself, puts your focus on to something else. So it is with the creative voice in the activity of singing. It means that you are responsive to the present moment, with no other aim than to be fully and sensitively alive and 'with the music' of the moment. This is something that you can learn to experience through exploring and discovering the voice alone.

SINGING YOUR OWN SONG

'The singing was the listening, the listening created the song.'
Chloë Goodchild, singer and voice teacher,
The Naked Voice: Journey to the Source of Sound, 1993

The most wonderful moment in your life may be when you give voice to your very own song. This does not have to be a song that you have carefully composed and written, but one that springs straight from your heart and soars out unplanned, composing itself as you sing it, and as you listen – a totally improvised song for yourself. Such songs bring together in a moment all the rich panoply of sounds and feelings your voice contains, and they need few or even no words. When you are sufficiently prepared, and allow yourself to follow the impulse, your voice will suddenly express, with natural musicality, all you feel and care about in the here and now. You may sing laments or songs of celebration, lullabies or blood-curdling warrior songs, you may move yourself to laughter or tears and find yourself including half-remembered snatches of opera or gospel. Melodies buried in your subconscious may suddenly emerge in this way, bringing with them both joy and sadness, releasing new energy into your voice and body – if you let them. Your voice may move from humour to pathos, from drama to comedy, from lyricism to fervour, as you follow the feeling, the moment. Anything could happen.

> *'You may say I'm a dreamer, but I'm not the only one.'*
> John Lennon, 'Imagine', 1971

BEAUTY AND THE BEAST

In such moments there will be no censoring, no exclusion; following your feeling, your listening and in particular the rhythms of your breath, you will risk all, beauty and apparent 'ugliness' weaving in and out of each other as you 'sing your heart out'. Such songs, sung for yourself, which sometimes last only a few minutes or even less, are 'of the moment' and carry your essence, but they can equally well form the basis for your own future compositions.

Once you have released your voice in this way, you will have found forever the source of song in yourself, and you can then begin to connect that source to other songs written and composed by other people.

THE DANCING VOICE

Jenny's voice was unknown territory to her until she started exploring sound as she had once explored movement. As a dancer she could express so much through her body, improvising and inventing all sorts of movements easily, but she had not yet made the same imaginative connection with her voice. Her body could move, but not her voice. One day, in a dancing and singing improvisation exercise, her voice 'took off'. She allowed her movements to follow the sounds and natural songs that flowed from her – and the sounds to follow the movement. Then she slowly stilled her dancing while continuing to give voice. She was able to 'follow' her voice from low, middle to high, up and down, improvising with different qualities and feelings of sound, sustained or staccato. Her voice had become a dancer, too.

Singing is to do with an inner movement of sound and breath that is akin to dance.

'VOICE DANCE' OR FREE VOCAL IMPROVISATION

'Voice dance' does not have to be reserved for dancers, or even for rehearsal studios: you could be driving happily along wide empty highways, or be by the sea. In fact, a background sound, like the wind in high trees, waves, or simply the drone of a car engine stops you thinking too much. Certain instruments can support you by providing a similar effect that helps you to liberate your voice and imagination. A friendly accordionist, jazz pianist or drummer could help you find and sustain the impulse needed to let your voice 'dance' free. You may equally well decide to find a soundproofed studio or room to enjoy fully the unique sound of your own dancing voice. If you record these sessions, use an ambient sound recorder rather than a hand-held microphone, so that you are not tempted to stand in front of an imaginary audience and 'perform' – yet.

In whichever situation, give yourself time to connect with your breath and body energies.

Voice dancing

* Preparation: remember the 'three keys' in the spine. Stretch. Shoulder rolls, 'snake', dance and vocalise freely as a cat to warm through your voice. MMO.

* Practise any of the suggested exercises from Parts 2 or 3.

* At the keyboard, sing one note at a time rather than sing/sliding. Use the single sung note as a springboard for your improvisation.

* Imagine yourself taking flight vocally from this one note, allowing your voice to leap or plunge, and to soar and glide where and how it wants to, in a free improvisation.

* Breathe as often as you like. Keep the connection between the in-breath and VOB. Let your listening be your guide. Follow your voice. When the quality of sound changes, go with the change, stay with the difficulties until sound and feeling flow again.

* Your 'voice dance' can range through the lower, middle and higher parts of your voice, and can include sing/slides, dialogue between different voices, rhythmical moments, animal sounds, textures – in fact, anything that suggests itself. Follow the impulse of the moment.

Remember: Breath is the food of song. Breathe when you need to.

Follow your voice

It is important to move away from the keyboard as soon as you have begun, and keep your body moving, however small the movement. Re-connecting with your own song through 'voice dance' is something you can return to again and again to refresh your imagination, to find inspiration and to hear – and enjoy – your own voice.

Old songs, new life

The ability to give voice to your own song will lead you closer to giving voice to other people's songs. You will be surer of the kind of music and style that corresponds to your inner music; your choices will be clearer. All this need not stop you exploring as much of the repertoire as you possibly can or want to. Once your whole voice spectrum is opened up, your appreciation of different singing styles will be deepened. You will begin to discover, through experimentation, that every style of singing has the potential to reveal further to you the hidden aspects of your own voice.

> 'The moon belongs to everyone, the best things in life are free,
> The stars belong to everyone, they gleam there for you and me.'
>
> Buddy De Sylva and Lew Brown,
> 'The Best Things in Life are Free', from *Good News*, 1927

Rather than searching through music shops for songs to practise, begin by searching in your own memory. Remember that our hearing up to the age of ten is acute; as children we soaked up every sound, every melody we ever heard. Jot down snatches, words you remember, the title of a song you love, the words of a nursery rhyme you sang as a child, or that you heard someone else singing. We know what we enjoy, musically, from a very early age – an opera-singing friend of mine says she remembers watching

Richard Strauss's opera *Salome* on television at the age of five – now, three decades later, she is singing arias from that opera herself. Another friend learned nearly all of Bob Dylan's songs by heart by the age of eight. Even if you can remember only the melody, the chorus, or the first verse, a song from memory can awaken your singing voice, and even bring surprising and encouraging reminders of an earlier ability. A little time spent actively searching, pencil and paper in hand, stimulates the singing centres in your mind and body.

People often don't sing for fear of getting it wrong. So, when you start, get it wrong. Break the rules. Sing those little songs from memory exactly as you like, without worrying about what it should, ought or must sound like. Breathe where and when you want to. Speed up. Slow down. Gabble. Shriek. Slur. Swoop. Get your voice moving. Sing them nice, sing them nasty, sing them clever, sing them daft. You may be surprised that when you begin to sing even the more tricky melodies in different ways, the melody suddenly comes out right. More so than if you laboriously and carefully try to 'get it right', or don't even give it a try. This is a playful preparation for adaptability and flexibility in your singing.

SING SOMETHING SIMPLE

Simple popular or folk songs allow you to experiment. They are not standing in judgement over you; they have no illustrious interpreters who have done it a hundred times better than you; the field is clear for you to explore. Singing something simple allows you to connect with the enjoyment of singing. When you can make a simple song interesting and fun for yourself, you will be able to do the same one day with a more complex song, for an audience. Practise with short simple songs with easy melodies and uncomplicated text.

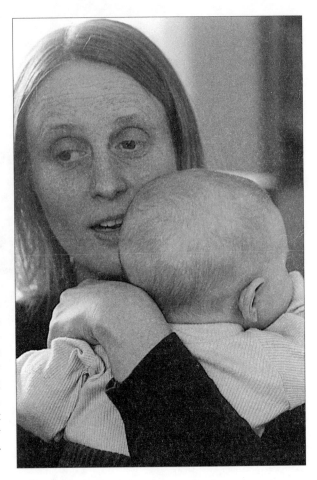

Changing your viewpoint

Familiar songs often become interesting again when we can sing from a new viewpoint. The following exercise will begin to help you loosen up your 'point of view'.

The singer Bobby McFerrin made the following song into a showstopper:

'Twinkle, twinkle, little star
How I wonder what you are!
Up above the world so high,
Like a diamond in the sky.

Twinkle, twinkle, little star,
How I wonder what you are!'

Jane Taylor, 'Twinkle, Twinkle, Little Star', 1806

Now see what you can do with it.

A dozen different ways to sing a simple song:

- pouting
- yawning
- gabbling
- on vowels only
- on consonants only
- rolling drunk
- really angry
- innocent
- questioning
- haughty
- naughty
- wild

Have fun!

This exercise will be referred to as: The 'Star Treatment'!

Many great singers give the impression of effortlessness, but we know, on the contrary, that it has taken them years of hard work to achieve the results we enjoy. You cannot eventually avoid the effort when you want to sing big songs for a big public, but you can remind yourself from time to time what it feels like to sing without trying.

WIDENING YOUR SONG SEARCH

The time has come to widen your search and discover a new repertoire. This is, and should be at this stage in your development, a very, very personal endeavour. Only you can know what appeals to you, and only when you choose a song you really like will you be prepared to make the effort involved in really learning to bring it to life. If it doesn't move you, how can you move it? You will be surprised to find how many song albums are available in music shops, libraries and, of course, on the Internet. You'll discover a vast and tempting selection to choose from, so it's best to have a few ideas of what kind of songs you are searching for.

SINGING SOMETHING FOR SOMEONE

You have come to the point where singing for yourself is not enough: you want to share, you need to share, you have something to give, you want to give it. All your explorations, discoveries and exercises now have a new focus: to sing something for someone.

All sorts of things can start to happen to even the most experienced singers when faced with an audience – even an audience of one. Let's go through the list:

- You forget the words.

- You lose the rhythm.

- You lose the beat.

- You come in too soon or too late.

- You start the song on the 'wrong' pitch – too high or too low.

- You run out of breath.

- You forget to do what you planned to do.

- Your mouth goes dry, your knees, or just one of them, starts to shake.

- You can't hear the accompanist.

- You lose contact with your body centres, you rush, and you trip, you falter and you stagger.

- You behave like a nervous and newly engaged waiter or waitress carrying an expensive meal from the kitchen to the client and, just about to bump into the irate boss, you drop the tray and get the sack!

Ask yourself: is a song something you have to serve up to an audience? Do you have to carry it, or, since you have made such a long and consistent effort to learn it, could it now carry you?

Facing the Music 2

STRUCTURE AND SECURITY

For the song to carry you, you have to know it, inside out. Learning a few basic things about music and text will give you the security you need to trust the 'wings of a song'.

This section will look at:

1 Text
2 Rhythm
3 Melody
4 Time signatures
5 Key choices

I. DISCOVERING THE MUSIC THROUGH THE TEXT

Bringing words to life

- You have chosen to sing a song you like, for the music and for what it says. Forget the melody for a while and concentrate on the music in the words – a little time spent looking at it word by word will give you even more pleasure when you come to sing it again.

- Write down or print out the full text of your song without any musical indications – as text. Read through your text as though each word is entirely separate.

- Don't search for meaning or feeling, and certainly don't look for any interpretation yet. If anything, read the text *against* the obvious interpretation, break it out of its clichés: shout it or whisper it, or giggle your way through.

- Taste the individual words one by one on their own sonorous merits, then put the text aside for a while and give it time to speak to you. You may be surprised by the way that certain words and phrases will float into your mind at moments when you are engaged with other things, bringing with them unexpected meanings.

- Read through your text as a poem, image by image and thought by thought, speaking it aloud without singing it. Take time.

One thought at a time

'You are speaking not your own thoughts, but someone else's which you must make your own . . . the secret of how to do this is so simple. Having spoken your thoughts, shut your mouth and allow the lungs gently to refill. Refuse to rush on. Intend only to live in the one thought – then perhaps decide to take yet another thought, and pause again. Try it.'

- This way of working with poetry, recommended by Sir George Trevelyan in his book *Magic Casements* (1980), gives time for each image of your text to come to life in your imagination.

- Try it with the following verse from Paul Simon's song: 'April, Come She Will' (1965).

- Read out loud, following the instructions given:

  'April, come she will,'
  > Pause, shut your mouth, allow the lungs gently to refill.
  'When streams are ripe and swelled with rain.'
  > Refuse to rush on.
  'May...' (wait) *'...she will stay.'*
  > Shut your mouth, and allow the lungs gently to refill.
  'Resting in my arms again.'

When you start singing a song that you have spoken in this way, you will find, more often than not, that you completely understand the pauses and rests included by the composer as part of the music. They will no longer be awkward, 'dead' moments you have to endure until you can make a sound again, but truly 'pregnant pauses'. You have relived the original inspiration for the song by going back to the image. You give the words time to release their images, and you give the images time to speak to you.

'Rhyme and rhythm are magic. They are the inner life and power of the poem,' wrote Sir George Trevelyan.

And the poem, or text, is the inner life and power of the song.

When you work through any text in this way you will avoid that most common of all pitfalls: anticipation. Anticipation means that we give away the final outcome of the song right from the start, as though we know what it is all about, the moment we start singing it. Of course we do know, but in order to bring it to life we have to relive each step of the story, as if we don't know. If you read your song text through slowly, image by image, shutting your mouth in between as recommended, you may be very surprised at the way the story comes through, very often not at all as you imagined it. The words and images themselves, together with the music, will tell you how the feelings are moving and changing, and what the song is about. You do not have to think it all out with your brain. When you give value to each image *as it comes*, you will be telling, then singing, the story as the person who is experiencing it – in the very moment, not as a past event.

> '. . . *her soul sings unencumbered*
> *Because the song's what makes her sing.*'

Fernando Pessoa (1888-1935), 'Harvest Woman'
(trans. Jonathan Griffin)

2. RHYTHM WITHOUT BLUES

A poetic text is very often the inspiration for the melody of a song. For this reason, if you give time to feeling the rhyme and rhythm through the spoken text, the melody will often fall into place more easily as a consequence. Words give rhythm, and rhythm gives life. Life has swing. Count Basie is reported to have said to a woman who asked him what was 'swing': 'If you don't know, lady, I can't tell you.' We've all got rhythm, and we can all get 'swing', although we may not think so. The body is full of the natural rhythms of breathing and of the pulsing of our hearts. We breathe in and we breathe out, the heart goes 'lub-dub, lub-dub, lub-dub, lub-dub'. Our daily speech is full of rhythms, whether we realise it or not. We live to the rhythm of time. We feel the hours, minutes and seconds as they tick by. Some people say we have an 'internal' clock. That is rhythm. We fall easily into natural rhythms while walking, running, dancing. We move from side to side, from foot to foot. That's a natural one-two marching rhythm. We tap and clap spontaneously when listening to music; we beat time. We are exhilarated by drumming rhythms that seem to release hidden sources of energy in us. We need rhythm. Most of the songs we sing organise this basic 'rhythm of life' into easily recognisable groups, such as, for instance, groups of two beats, or the three beats of a waltz, or four beats and so on. Musical rhythm is inspired by, and underpins, the song text itself.

> *'The blues ain't nothing but a pain in your heart,*
> *When you get a bad start, when you and your man have to part,*
> *I ain't gonna just sit around and cry,*
> *I know I won't die, 'cos I love him.'*

Billie Holiday and Herbie Nichols, 'Lady Sings the Blues', 1956

If your ambition is to sing blues, there is absolutely no substitute for listening to blues rhythms, in whatever shape or form, over and over again until you get to feel them in your own bloodstream, until they're coming out of every pore in your body. Whatever the rhythm that gets you tapping and clapping, listen to it actively; sing along with it; move to it; dance to it. Practising and gaining confidence in as many different rhythms as possible will release more confidence in your voice, and vice-versa. Rhythm is the litmus test for energy, and energy is an essential ingredient of rhythm. Get energy and you'll have fewer problems with rhythm. Energy low? You lose the beat. Work at rhythm, get that beat – you get energy. More and more of it. Slow, fast – it doesn't matter; if the energy is low, you'll be late for the beat. If it's there you can learn to channel it, hold it, like holding a team of horses. When you get into the rhythm, there's the energy. When you work with MMO, through the body, breath and feeling, there's the energy – and readiness to 'get' the beat.

> *'Energy is eternal delight.'*
> William Blake, *The Marriage of Heaven and Hell*, 1790

Finding the rhythm (15 minutes)

- Put on some music you enjoy. If you have an electronic keyboard, go through every one of the hundred rhythms it usually offers, from samba to mazurka. You will learn a lot!

- Move around as you listen. Try to feel the rhythm of your chosen piece of music, listening for the main 'down beat'.

- Step in time, clap in time. Count out the rhythm on your fingers; improvise a dance in rhythm to the music. Move.

- Sing out loud along with the music, counting the beats: 1-2-3-4, or 1-2-3, or 1-2, 1-2.

- Find the song that has been giving you rhythm problems. Work at it again. Take one phrase. Repeat it until you are satisfied, until you feel it is right. If you are dissatisfied, find a musician friend to help you. Then take the next phrase – and the next.

3. MEMORY AND MELODY

The words and the rhythm combined represent a good half of the 'melody' of a song. Give yourself as long as you need to memorise it. There are no rules: no one ever said you should be able to get it right first go. Take the time *you* need. The following points may help you in the process.

Every melody has a form, or structure. The very simplest are composed of one or two basic musical ideas that repeat themselves for as many verses as there are in the song. An example is the song: 'When Irish Eyes are Smiling': the verse has one melody and the chorus another, and within the chorus melody there is a repetition and a simple change to draw the song to a close. If you know it, sing it through:

A *'When Irish eyes are smiling, sure it's like a morn in Spring,*
B *In the lilt of Irish laughter, you can hear the angels sing,*
C *When Irish hearts are happy, all the world seems bright and gay,*
D *And when Irish eyes are smiling, sure they steal your heart away!'*

Chauncey Olcott and George Graff, Jr.,
'When Irish Eyes are Smiling', 1912

In such simple songs, there is usually one melody line for the story and another for the chorus, or one melody for an introduction, then another for the main theme. Go through the song you have chosen to sing, and try and discern where the melody repeats itself – and where, how, and how often it changes. You may discover, as in some Beatles songs, a structure that could be marked: A.B.C. –

three different melodies that are then repeated in the same order. The famous song 'Help!' by The Beatles has the structure: A.B.C.-B.C.-B.C. Working out the structure of the melody by listening to a recording of the song can be helpful at this point, especially if you've written down the text beforehand, and keep a pencil handy!

> *'When I was younger, so much younger than today,*
> *I never needed anybody's help in any way.'*

Lennon/McCartney, 'Help!', 1965

Calling for help

The best way to learn the melody of your song is *not* by listening to tip-top professional recordings, with complex harmonies that can confuse your ear, but by finding a friendly pianist to guide you through it (if you cannot play the piano yourself, of course). Where do you find a pianist? Ask at your local music college or school; put an advertisement in the local paper; ask around: let people know you are looking. Once you have found your pianist ask him or her to make you a working tape as well. Ask them to play the *right hand only* for your recording. Pianists love to put in the left hand accompaniments, without which, for them, the music is not the music; but that may confuse you, until your ear grows accustomed to chord changes. If possible, work out the rhythm and pace you need; alternatively, ask your pianist to play the rhythm indicated at a slightly slower tempo (speed) than the one suggested. This working tape is now a useful tool, that you can listen to over and over again until you are familiar with the melody, going over the tricky patches as often as you need. As you begin to feel confident of the melody, you can put the recording aside, as you should also try to put the written text aside, trusting your memory and repeating both text and melody over to yourself silently or vocally whenever you can. Only in this way can you begin to make the song 'your own'. This cannot happen while it is still partly on the page or in your tape-recorder.

Being on time

Being 'on time' is a virtue that music gradually teaches us.

The hallmark of a professional musician is that he or she is never late – at least for the beat. Being 'on time' means being in time with your accompanist and starting to sing at the right moment: on the beat. Learning to 'come in' on time as you practise your song with an accompanist builds up that vital sense of structure that will help you eventually overcome nerves. 'Coming in on time' is like singing on the note, it is something that gives you objectivity. Practise by counting on your fingers, by tapping your foot, by clapping your hands, anything to help you eventually feel, without counting, the number of beats that underlie the musical introduction to your song and lead to the 'down-beat', or 'up-beat' where your voice joins the music. Then learn to sing the melody of the musical introduction without actually counting, and try to *feel the beat* through your whole body. Move around and test yourself again and again on just coming in on time.

> *'The essential note-to- note structure is only part of the music. For between*
> *and around these notes, so to speak, lies a vast domain of interpretive*
> *possibility, in which you can choose to play faster or slower, louder or softer,*
> *to phrase or articulate one way or another . . . it is what makes your performance*
> *individualistic, drab, eccentric, emotionally self indulgent or just plain brilliant.'*

Nicolas Cook, *Music: A Very Short Introduction*, 1998

Small details that make a big difference

Rhythm, tempo, dynamics, loudness, inflexion, softness and phrasing are all aspects of a song that you can work on to leave your own personal signature. But first you have to be aware of the composer's signatures.

4. TIME SIGNATURES

Time signatures have as much to with the rhythm as with the speed of a piece of music. When you know the melody and rhythm of a song you will have fun playing with pace or tempo. Popular music scores usually carry suggestions such as 'brightly', 'moderately', 'lively', 'briskly', 'at walking pace'. The pace or speed of a song is linked to the feeling or mood, and the important thing to re-member is that it is *elastic*. You can modify the pace; you can speed up and slow down within the overall structure to suit your imagination and the prompting of the text. But you have to keep an underlying sense of the 'beat' all the time – a slow waltz is still a waltz: 1-2-3, 1-2-3, 1-2-3. This is important when you are singing solo, whether with accompaniment or without ('a cappella').

5. KEY SIGNATURES

Piano keys, keyboards, keys as places in your spine – where will it all end? Now another key: the key signature. When a composer writes a piece of music he/she gives it a time signature and a 'key' signature. From these two signatures you can learn something of the composer's intended rhythm, pace, and mood. The 'key signature' determines the mood, or atmosphere, of a song, whether major or minor. The song 'Ev'ry Time We Say Goodbye', from the musical *The Seven Lively Arts* by Cole Porter (1944), is interesting for its change of key from major to minor, which expresses exactly the mood of the singer, from happiness at being with the lover to sadness at parting. The key signature determines the scale of notes: how many tones, how many half-tones (semitones) and in what order, how many 'sharpened' tones, how many 'flattened'. All this adds up to a particular flavour, atmosphere and musical signature or sound.

'Tempo di-sturb de neighbours'

You may learn to identify and name the particular sound of each key, from C major to G minor for instance, but you can sing well without this specific knowledge as long as you recognise when a key actually changes in a piece of music (as in the Cole Porter song above).

Choices of tempo and dynamics are often indicated by a written instruction as well, such as 'softly' or 'growing louder' or the Italian 'pianissimo' for very softly. Fats Waller has a good one: 'Tempo di-sturb de neighbours' for a song called 'The Joint is Jumpin''. Check the composer's instructions on any musical score you might be working from: you will find it helps!

Making changes

The thing to remember about musical keys of both time and mood is that, at least for popular music, they are merely indications or suggestions about how the person who wrote the music would like it to be performed, and they can be changed.

Transposition, or useful moves

The musical 'key', which can be changed to suit your voice, gives the starting note for your song. This is most relevant if you are singing with an accompanist. Because you need to sing in harmony when you are accompanied, you and your accompanist need to agree on this one small point! Most musicians love to try out different keys – 'transposing', as it is called, up, or down; and will be delighted that you are willing to sing in different areas of your voice range. The key signature can be transposed, or moved to the same mood starting on a different note. If the starting note is too high for you, you are unlikely to be able to sing the higher notes of the song. So you can transpose the song down – or vice-versa. Thanks to electronic keyboards, pianists can now transpose the written key of a song automatically, and give the information to the rest of the band. You don't know how lucky you are. Whole careers have foundered on this issue alone! The singer now calls the tune: the soloist no longer has to sing in discomfort merely because 'that is where it's written'. The best key is the one that enables you to express the feeling of the song the way you want to, and are able to. Karaoke singers take note: you don't have to be forced into singing too low, or too high. Just ask – change the key please! Once you have agreed on the key, you will have help in recognising your starting note from the accompanist's musical introduction. Your ear training will help you with this step, and you and your accompanist will work together. Never be afraid to admit difficulty, or to ask for as much practice time as you need, until *you* feel secure. Are you getting the picture? *You* set the tempo and *you* choose the key.

Song-Learning Checklist

Dry mouth, shaking knees, nausea, fear, stage fright: one or all may come to meet you when you go out to meet any audience, whether large or small, friendly or unknown. The only way to overcome these things, said a singer friend of mine, is to sing for an audience often – do more of it! However, the better prepared you are each time, the less your knees will shake.

Go through the following list as a preparation:

1 **Facing the music:**
   - **Melodic structure or form**
   - **Key signature:** Highest note and lowest note (range)
   - **First interval**
   - **Rhythm/Tempo**

2 **Exploring the text:**
   - **Image by image**
   - **What are you singing about?**
   - **Who is singing?** Choice of character or viewpoint
   - **Who are you singing to?** Choice of focus – inner or outer
   - **Action:** Decisions about movement, dance or gesture

FINDING THE FEELING

When you first rehearse your song, you do not have to have *the* feeling, but very soon, for the song to come alive at all, you do have to have *a* feeling. Rather than preparing yourself carefully to withstand or ignore any feelings, from sorrow to anger, that might 'pop out' when you open your mouth to sing and sabotage you on your big day, it is better to meet them in advance as you practise. Keep some paper handkerchiefs handy; get to know what these feelings do to your breathing, and what they sound like 'in rehearsal'! Repeat the 'Star Treatment' exercise (page 177) to help you explore the feelings that are right for you *and* for the song. Sing through your song as an 'animal aria', like a cat or a wolf. Give the 'chords of emotion' a bit of freedom.

MEETING THE MUSICIANS

There may come a moment when your confidence is high, you find yourself in a friendly club, you have a few songs ready and you want to sing with a band. A few words of warning. When you join other musicians, they expect you to be just like them – a musician first, not a singer. So if, after you have had a wonderful time, sung your heart out and made heaps of friends in the audience, one or several of the musicians look at you a trifle dismissively and say, 'you don't sing in time', or 'you lose the beat' or 'your rhythm needs smartening up', don't take it personally; don't be disheartened, and most of all don't give up: you'll never survive if you do.

> *'Nothing's impossible I have found, for when my chin is on the ground,*
> *I pick myself up, dust myself off, start all over again.'*

> Dorothy Fields, 'Pick Yourself Up', from *Swing Time*, 1936

To most musicians, the singer is, to all intents and purposes, just another instrumentalist who had better be, like them (or like they try to be), on time, on pitch, and on the beat. Most musicians have, as it were, given their voices to their instruments, and they have trained and practised arduously so that they can play in tune, in rhythm, on the beat, in time and in harmony with the other musicians. They will expect you to be able to do the same. What might appear as criticism from them is often just an evaluation, from one musician to another: a technical point, of a kind they are constantly working on, not a devaluation of you – or of your voice. Also, most semi-professional or amateur musicians who play in clubs in the evenings or at weekends are doing so to relax and have a good time. Even if they knew how to help an enthusiastic fledgling singer, they probably wouldn't want to – that is not what they are there for. So bear that in mind: if you tried once and were not up to standard, and the musicians were possibly a bit impatient, go back to the piano, polish up one or two songs you feel fully confident about, get them on pitch, on the beat and in rhythm, and then: 'take a deep breath, pick yourself up, dust yourself off, and start all over again.'

Summary of Part Five

- Creative singing means that you are totally present and responsive to the moment and able to call on any part of your voice to express *what* you want, *how* you want.

- Finding the 'source' of song in yourself helps you to sing other people's songs better.

- Your voice can be a dancer, too.

- Break the rules. Experiment. There are many ways to sing a song.

- Could the song 'carry' you?

- There are certain essentials you need to know to help give new life to old songs.

- When you give life to a song, the song will give life to you.

SIX

The Singer and the Song

'Si se calla el cantor calla la vida
porque la vida, la vida misma es todo un canto.'

[*'When the singer falls silent, life falls silent,*
for life, life itself, is as a song.']

Horacio Guarany, 'Si se calla el cantor',
performed by Mercedes Sosa, 1973

SIX

The Singer and the Song

Facing the Audience

Here is the magic: there can be no song without a singer, and no singer without
a song. The singer must give voice and life to the song, and then the song will
give life and meaning to the singer. Sooner or later, a singer with a song will be
heard, if only by an audience of one. Even if the audience numbers a thousand,
the singer may still feel that what matters is to be truly listened to by just one
person. This is how you begin – by singing for yourselves, then for someone
else, and then gradually gaining the courage to sing for more and more people,
until you have a 'public'. Then, if you eventually get to record your voice on a
CD, you will still mostly be singing for just one person, alone with their stereo,
listening to and being captivated by the singer and the song. Once you have
discovered and developed the ability to sing to and for one person, you can sing
for a thousand. If that indispensable combination of luck and hard work leads
you to build up a relationship with an audience, you will have a totally new
dynamic to work with – not just the rapport between yourself and your song,
but also that between singer, song and audience.

AN INTENSE RELATIONSHIP

The demands of this relationship are poignantly described in the film *I Could
Go On Singing* (1963), starring Judy Garland and Dirk Bogarde. It's well worth
seeking out and watching, if only for one amazing and touching scene between
these two actors. In a short piece of dialogue they make a very interesting
revelation about a singer's motivation, as well as creating a high point of
emotional intensity. Garland plays herself as a singer about to make a comeback
after a long professional break; Bogarde plays her ex-husband and only true
friend. For numerous personal reasons she has kept her audience waiting, and
is in a state of great vulnerability.

D.B. *Listen! They're waiting.*

J.G. *I don't care if they're fasting! Just let them wait. I can't be spread so thin. It's
just not worth all the deaths that I have to die.*

D.B. *You have a show tonight.*

J.G. *D'you think you can make me sing? You can get me there, but can you make me sing? I sing for myself. I sing when I want to, whenever I want to. Just for me. I sing for my own pleasure. Do you understand that?*

D.B. (with intensity) *Yes, I do, just hang on to that, will you? Just hang on . . .*

Then she strides on stage to thunderous applause, and delivers!

Having Dirk Bogarde or some other screen idol to hold your hand is not a bad plan when the prospect is scary! Singers often have to go out on stage alone, and no one can sing for you, but the presence of a friend to give you a hug or a smile before you meet an audience, however friendly, is probably one of the greatest voice warm-ups possible.

A FORM OF DIALOGUE

The following insight into the singer/song/audience rapport may be especially useful to the new, inexperienced singer.

'The relationship is a dialogue,' a friend told me, 'so listen to the audience as much as you expect them to listen to you, especially before you start. Listen calmly, and in a friendly way, *and wait until they are ready to listen to you.*'

As good a moment as any to remember the 'three keys' in your backbone, and to breathe from your feet upwards.

Real 'presence' comes only when it has been cultivated all the time, as much in our daily lives and contact with others as on the stage.

'Presence' is to do with having a sense of theatre without being 'theatrical'.

This means cultivating a sense of what is appropriate to the moment, the people, the place and the circumstances.

PRESENCE, PRESENTATION AND FOCUS
ONE MORE KEY

'The key to happiness is not to be so self-involved.'
Bette Midler, American singer and actress

This advice could just as well apply to the aspiration to 'presence'. Singing has the power to bring us totally into the moment, which means being less self-involved

and focusing more on something other than ourselves. Singing requiresus to live in 'the now'. Every song has to be sung as though for the first time, with you as both composer and poet. Your task is to re-invent the song each time you sing it – vocally, expressively and bodily. This becomes easy when you are truly living in 'the now', able to connect all you have learned with the journey on which each song takes you. For this reason, too much planning or setting of moves and gestures in advance can be a trap that prevents you from re-creating the song in the moment.

> *'I never sing a song the same way twice;*
> *everything depends on how I feel in the moment.'*
> Ray Charles, American soul singer

However, until we get to those dizzy heights it is as well to have both aim and direction: know where you are going, and what you have to do – even if you end up not doing it.

Most of all, presence is to do with being prepared. As the saying goes: You can get away with charm for the first five minutes – after that, you'd better know something!

EDD   (Explore, Discover, Develop)

MMO   (Muscles, Mobility and Openness)

VOB   (Vibrating Out-Breath)

MVA   (Multi-Variable Aperture) and

PMP   (Practice Makes Perfect)

In the film *Latchmo Drom* (1993), a musical history of the Tzigane people, directed by Tony Gatlif, a young gypsy boy sings as he walks alongside the family caravan that is travelling across the Indian desert; the sound of his singing obviously gives him and his people the courage to cross the arid wasteland. His voice is firm and strong, his message reaches us beyond the words he uses, and quite clearly he is proud to be filmed while singing: in other words, he has presence – a sense of 'the theatre of the moment'.

Working with Supportive Group Feedback

The new singer, of whatever age, needs encouraging support and intelligent feedback from a friendly audience before braving an unknown public. Such support can be found through working regularly with a teacher, singing with a good choir, attending voice workshops, or creating your own small singing group. A group such as this can provide a small, friendly and constructive audience for its members. In this way, you can begin to work with 'group feedback'. In the hope that you will one day find a singing group to work with, here are a few insights that I have gained from this way of working.

In my own workshop sessions I encourage students to give each other positive and creative feedback, to watch each other and try to understand what it is that engages the listener and makes them listen. Each student prepares a song in advance, in lessons and practice sessions. The group workshop then provides an opportunity for the singer to experience an 'audience', and to give a small performance of the song in a secure and friendly setting, giving the singer an opportunity to get closer to answering those two most important questions:

- What are you singing about?
- Who are you singing to?

The honest response to such questions might produce such simple answers as: 'I'm singing to hear the sound of my voice', and: 'I'm singing to you.' Sometimes, however, we do not realise or acknowledge the fact that, though we seem to be singing to someone else, we are singing to ourselves, and we are singing about something personal that the song has touched on. To arrive at a clearer understanding of what we are singing about, and to whom we are singing, we need feedback from our listeners.

We work only with constructive positive comment that allows the vision of the singer's voice and the song to expand rather than diminish.

WHAT COMES ACROSS?

Not what you think you did.

Not what you say you did.

But what you actually did.

And what I, the listener and observer, experienced as a result.

Helpful feedback is the kind that gives the singer an idea of what actually came across – not what ought to have come across, or could/should have come across. It is not necessarily a moment for engaging in musical evaluation, for picking the singer up on rhythm and beat. The task of 'facing an audience' brings enough uncertainties in itself, quite apart from the technical problems that can be addressed elsewhere. Thinking about this approach, it is clear that certain kinds of comment are not really constructive or useful: 'I think so-and-so should have put more emphasis on the last line of the song,' or: 'I thought it was a pity so-and-so didn't look at us,' or: 'He missed the beat,' or: 'It would have been better if she/he had done such and such.' Comments like this tend to start tiring discussions that sap everyone's energy and enthusiasm.

INVOLVED LISTENING

Feedback from friends, in an attentive and constructive atmosphere, is far more helpful than misplaced critical evaluation. Members of the group are asked to be an 'active audience'. This implies a certain way of sitting, as well as the willingness to maintain a positive and friendly expression – they are not just waiting passively to be entertained, but are taking part in the process of helping the singer to develop and improve his or her performance. As one student jokingly put it: 'No matter what or how I sing, you will enjoy it – and you will show it!'

A CLEAR MIRROR REFLECTION

The class are encouraged to act as a mirror, 'feeding back' to the performer what they actually heard, felt and saw, and thus helping the singer know what comes across. The best way to give this kind of reflection is to use metaphor. I ask the class audience to allow images to come to them while the singer is singing, so that afterwards they are ready to comment. Their responses some-times take the form of one word only: for example, 'gutsy', 'exciting', 'spring-like', 'brave' or 'vulnerable'. Sometimes the singer may have intended a wild performance, but everyone's feedback tells them how sweet, nice and kind they were. If a group member says things like: 'You should have been nastier', or: 'Why did you smile so much?' the singer will then try and be 'nastier', or smile less, to please that person – or they may even withdraw from the challenge altogether. The idea is to aim for the delicate balance between singer and group audience that allows each singer to become more consciously aware of what is being received, and then search for their own creative response.

THE MEANING OF 'GOOD'

We do make value judgements, of course, but the important thing is to keep them related to an ongoing process. One day a student said to me, 'Finally, I understand what you mean when you say "That's good": you mean it's good for me right now, not in comparison with any other so-called objective standards.'

Ahhh! When we listen in a non-judgemental way, we always hear what is 'good' in the moment, because it's *always* possible to feel and hear a genuine intention, expressed by voice and body together. You can always hear when the singer is connecting thought, feeling, body and imagination 'here and now', in the moment, and not just churning out an old, tired idea. Every time a singer makes those vital connections, the ability to do it again is strengthened: that's half the battle of becoming professional.

TELLING STORIES

Singing is about giving life to stories, feelings and images through voice and music: when these are coming over, you are communicating well, and your singing is getting good – you are on the way! This is an example of one of the best pieces of feedback I have heard recently: 'I was just so captivated by what she was singing about, I forgot all about her voice!'

Ten Short Voice Stories

These ten stories offer you glimpses into some of my individual and group workshop lessons, in which I explore the voice and guide students towards ways of finding new energy and interpretative ideas for their singing. I have, for reasons of confidentiality, changed the names and personal details, but the stories are essentially true, noted down by me after class.

Each voice, and therefore each lesson, is unique. Every lesson is determined by the infinite variations of character and circumstances present. I hope this section, together with the other parts of the book, will inspire you to trust your own imagination and creativity, to listen without a plan, to hear what is 'there', and to take the risk of exploring the unknown. If you approach your singing in this way, you will never be disappointed. Above all, I hope the examples will inspire you to seek out similar opportunities where, in a supportive and creative setting, you can search and explore your own singing body and moving voice.

Each story starts from 'where we are now', in the belief that everyone, from the most timid newcomer to the experienced professional, has somewhere to go.

I. PETER

Peter is eighteen, a tall, energetic, good-natured and hard-working young actor. What can I teach him in an hour that might help him? What does he want to learn?

'How it all works,' he says.

'Where does your voice come from?' I ask.

He waves his hands around vaguely, and looks a little confused.

'The lungs?'

'Yes, sort of; anywhere else?'

Again, the hands wave around.

'Well, something in here – ' indicating his throat, 'the vocal cords?'

'Yes – and how do you make sound?'

'I haven't really thought about it.'

I tell Peter about the three structures in the body that relate to making sound: the power producer, the place where sound is initiated, and the resonating centres in the chest and head. I remind him about the 'three keys' in the backbone. Through simple exercises we explore how he can use his body to create, increase and sustain sound, and how giving each sound a clear intention brings it immediately to life.

At the end of the one-hour lesson, he can relate the different qualities of sound he is making spontaneously to motivation, body posture, openness, and the movement of his chest, neck and jaw.

'Where did the time go?' he asks, 'I never thought just making sounds could be so much fun.'

'Remember what you did; practise it a bit,' I tell him. 'I want to awaken your curiosity about where your voice comes from, and what it is capable of doing. Listen to voices, think about resonance; notice how you move and how you breathe.'

'And then we'll continue?' he asks.

'Sure.'

2. STRIKING GOLD

Naomi is married to an enthusiastic amateur singer who is a member of two or three choirs and opera choruses. Not only has she herself been kept in the shade as a person: her own voice, too, has been more or less extinguished by her husband's 'expert' singing, which he developed at an early age as a choirboy. Now in her early forties, Naomi has a warm speaking voice, deep and mature, the kind of voice that fills easily with emotion. And there is a lot of emotion. She tells me how, when she was younger, she had a reputation in her college for singing music-hall songs with a great sense of comedy – but quickly adds, 'I can't sing them any more.'

'Let's try,' I invite her.

'No, really – I don't dare, I haven't sung for so long; I wouldn't trust my voice, I'd prefer to just explore.'

I play Middle C and invite her to search for a pleasurable, easy sound on an open 'Ah', immediately after taking an in-breath, without pausing, pretending at the same time that she is having a shower and giving herself an all-over scrub.

At a certain pitch she stops, saying that her throat is constricted, that she can't go on. I ask her to sing down a few notes to the frequencies where she had felt more comfortable, like getting back to 'base'. Then we climb again, note by note. But each time we near a particular note, somewhere within the octave above Middle C, the tightening in the throat reappears. Singing more and more softly, she is gradually able to approach the difficult area again.

'Do you want to stop?'

'No, I want to go on.'

'How do you feel?'

'I feel as though I've reached the edge of something – I don't know what.'

Her classmates are listening attentively, and when asked for feedback, one group member says that the sound of Naomi's voice had made her think spontaneously of molten lava.

'What do you think about that?' I ask Naomi.

'Sounds a bit hot.'

'Shall we try it?'

'Mud would be better.'

'Mud? Why not? "Mud, mud, glorious mud"!'

A few minutes of exploring the image and sound of 'mud' follow, which help Naomi's throat to relax. Her sense of humour leads her to play with different qualities of sound. The word is easy to sing, and its repetition begins to bring energy into her voice – an energy that has previously been lacking. Her face becomes alive and animated, and she begins to change expression with each new note, gradually releasing her jaw and moving her facial muscles. With her renewed confidence, she suddenly volunteers a rather tepid 'lava'. We play between 'lava' and 'mud' for a while, varying the pitch – up a note, then down a note: 'mud', 'lava'; words with very different sounds and associations.

Then the energy bursts out and the voice leaps from its bounds, raging like a torrent.

'On the note!'

'Hot lava!'

She sings from the middle part of her voice: 'Hot LAAAAVA!'

That word, 'lava', and the powerful images it holds for her, have the potential to wash away years of resentment about having her voice stifled, strangled and muted by the 'singer in the family'.

As we can see from this lesson, the opportunity to access vocal power comes from establishing a relationship between that emotional source of energy and the musical note.

Naomi's audience are watching her open-mouthed, leaning forward and willing her to continue as we edge that lava flow note by note towards the 'tight' area that had been a problem for her voice earlier in the lesson.

'Do you want to go on?'

She nods. Her voice, gaining power, resonance, vibrancy and animal energy, engages with her body to transform her suddenly from a tired housewife, mother and secretary into a strong and very vibrant woman.

The sound of Naomi's voice contains the primitive energy of a howl, a cry, a wound: keeping it anchored to the musical note enables her to connect with her frustration and rage in a creative way that suddenly carries her voice through the 'lava stream' and into a miraculously clear, warm golden sound which holds all her maturity, womanhood, generosity and warmth. There are tears, then laughter, then a totally theatrical roar; more laughter, smiles: her face is red and glowing, her body alive.

'What will you sing for us now?' I ask her.

'"Hallelujah"! "Roll out the Barrel"! "Joshua, Joshua"! "My Old Man Said Follow the Van"! My voice is still there!'

3. LASZLO

Laszlo is a recent drama school graduate. You should have seen him in a running exercise given earlier in the workshop – he was flying, with arms spread and limbs loose, filling the stage! He was full of strength, vigour, lightness, really free and happy, loving it. Now he sings. This is when the flying stops. He has a well-trained but weary voice. It is good, but I can't hear him enjoying or taking pride in either his skill, his expression or his power. He is just 'doing it'. He's too clever, almost. 'Been there, done that.'

'Let's take your voice back to the wilds for a while,' I suggest. 'Improvise with simple, open vowel sounds, and use them to tame a wild animal. Move around the room. Let your imagination provide the animal, bird or any non-human beast: call, cajole, try to get near enough, then decide what happens.'

Many imaginary animals lead him this way and that round the room. His voice and body gradually become more alive and engaged. He crouches by a chair and half-sings, half-whispers. He becomes a young hunter, and his cries are full of colour and expression. Then he takes an imaginary small bird into his cupped hands and lets it flutter to the sound of his voice against his breast. This is an extraordinary small and fragile sound. It seems to contain so much of Laszlo. It is as though suddenly he has once again made contact with a part of his voice that has escaped formal training.

'Start your song again from this "small bird" feeling,' I suggest, 'and see where the bird flies you to . . . '

One of the positive things about any artistic training is that it teaches the ability to concentrate and focus, to 'hold', 'stay' and 'go' with new sensations. Laszlo has these abilities. The song soars.

'That was new,' he says, 'I'm sweating!'

4. MALIN EXPLORES THE 'LAND' OF HER VOICE

In his book *The Songlines* (1987), Bruce Chatwin describes how the Aboriginals could not believe the country existed until they could see and sing it. The land must first exist as a concept in the mind, then it must be sung and only then can it be said to exist. This is the inspiration for the following 'lesson'.

Malin, in her early twenties, is a member of a class that has followed an eight-week training course in which we have covered much of the ground described in this text, discovering, exploring and developing from the basics upwards. This session records her first 'imaginative' exploration of her voice. Malin had once enjoyed singing, 'especially when I was a child,' she says, and since then has sung from time to time; but something has damaged her confidence, and she has lost the enjoyment of her own voice, and with it, the pleasure of singing. She is now prepared to approach her voice from the imaginative angle, rather than the physical.

A 'voice' journey

We take the words 'my land' as a stepping-stone to the imagination, and think of ourselves setting off on a journey of discovery into the voice. Any difficulties, problems or blocks we encounter are to be transformed into features of an imaginary landscape, which we will listen to and look at with curiosity. What is the sound about – what does it suggest? The words 'my land' have the advantage of open vowels and a singing consonant at the end: 'n'. Malin sings out the phrase, starting from the Middle C of the keyboard:

'Maaaaeeeyee Laaaannnnd!'

Entering with her into the spirit of the exercise, as though following her on her journey, I ask her to describe where she is. Already her imagination was actively connecting with her voice. She replies:

'On a mountain in the North; I've never actually been there, but I know it's a beautiful region.'

I play another note in the middle of the keyboard. She repeats 'my land', her voice confident and grounded, as though she has indeed found 'her land'.

'Now?' I ask.

'Yes, I'm on a mountain.'

'Do you like it?'

'Yes, very much.'

'Sing the words again,' I ask.

We listen to changes in vocal quality on each note, and observe them without judgement.

'What does that sound feel like to you? Familiar or unfamiliar? Is it still your land?'

Each note she sings is listened to intently and actively by me, Malin herself and the rest of the class. The quality of listening from the group is helping Malin to hear herself. The ability to both hear and feel, fundamental to the process of discovering and training our vocal powers, develops best when we are given time, space, concentration and active, non-judgemental listening by others.

Rough places

The resonance in Malin's voice deepens and swells as we continue. She sings two or three more notes, travelling upwards in pitch, with the same feeling of enjoyment. Then the quality of the sound changes again. It is less full, and has a touch of sadness.

'Where are you now?'

'In a forest.'

'And the sadness? Does it make you feel sad?'

'Yes, a bit.'

'It's all right to feel the sadness,' I tell her, 'but keep contact with your imagination, and let your voice describe the place and your feeling. We are sometimes sad when we return to places we left a long time ago, like places of childhood that we have had to leave, or parts of our voices that we have forgotten or neglected. Again.'

Once again she sings out the words 'my land'. The strain is evident.

'Where are you now?'

'Well, I can see the forest – but I can't seem to get into it; I want to get into it, but there's something in the way.' She indicates her throat.

'Forget your throat. Stay with the image. Let's look at whatever is in the way through the image – maybe a stream to cross, or stony ground? . . . Again. Gently . . . give the difficulty a voice.'

This time, because the 'obstacle' is accepted as part of the image, and voiced – crackles and all – there is no more strain in her voice; there is a change in quality, and again suddenly more resonance. New spaces open up. She continues to sing easily for four or five notes higher up the scale, and again there is a new change in texture and resonance.

'What is that?'

'There's a large stone in my landscape now.'

'Give the stone a voice,' I suggest.

She sings, and then dimples.

'I feel like a little girl.'

'Sing like a little girl singing to your stone.'

'My st–o–ne.' she sings in a small high voice. I play the same note an octave lower down. 'Now,' I suggest, 'sing "here I am" – as the stone – on the lower note.'

There follows a magical dialogue between the little girl and the stone, each part of her voice an octave apart and different in quality, clear and unforced. Then yet another quality comes through.

'What's happening now?'

'It's night-time.'

'Sing on the words "It's night-time": bring out that new soft quality in your voice.'

Now Malin has three clearly different vocal qualities: they relate to the stone, to the little girl – in the higher register – and to night-time, a second texture on the same note as the 'stone' sound, in the deeper part of her voice.

As the note on which she sings the word 'night' rises in pitch, I suggest that she think of stars, then play a note a full octave above what she had sung. 'Sing "I am a star",' I suggest.

Her voice rings out clearly, resonantly, vibrating on the high note, higher and higher, a soft beauty. She beams. I suggest she moves freely from one quality to the other, through the low, middle and high parts of her voice, still locating the sound firmly within the images that have emerged.

'From here you can create or improvise a melody about the stone, yourself, the night and the stars. Change the vowel sounds as you feel like.'

Both Malin's melody and her whole being become full and expressive: her voice rises and falls, full of feeling and magic. We listen, entranced, until she brings her song to its close.

Malin's experience

I showed my notes from the lesson to Malin, and ask her if she would write down her own account, making her own comments. Her only remark is one of amazement that the qualities she felt in her voice could also be so clearly heard by others. Here is her account of her 'Voice Journey':

> '*I am on a mountain in the North, where I have never been. It is beautiful. This is my land, and I'm proud of it. It is "my beautiful land". I'm hesitating about going down the mountain towards the forest. I feel a bit sad about confronting it, but I don't know why. I go slowly down the mountain. Now I enter the forest, and I recognise it. This is in the South: it's the forest where I used to play in the summer as a child. I feel very sad and also very happy to be here again – the mixed emotions make me cry. I go deeper into the forest and see a big stone. I recognise it. It is a very big, flat stone, near where I, my brother and my cousins used to build tree houses. It is "my stone". I sit on it. Now I am a little girl, dressed in white. The stone has its own voice, it says "here am I" – I speak to the stone, which is big, heavy and safe.*
>
> *It turns to night. I am alone on the stone. I look up into the sky. The night is big and dark, and the stars are plentiful. I am small and bright in my white dress. "I am a star." I sing to the stars. I can reach up to them with my voice. My voice is like a clear line, or thin beam, up to the stars. I feel lonely – happy, but lonely. I am unhappy in a happy way.*
>
> *I didn't know that I could sing this beautifully. My voice is strong and clear, and vibrates in a way I have never heard before.*'

In this journey, Malin is learning to let her voice both stimulate and follow her imagination. As the imagination gradually takes over as a guide, mental images or concepts begin to shape the sound, and the voice, like the Aboriginal land, is truly sung into existence.

5. BOB'S NEW 'WOMAN'

Bob is an active member of an amateur musical-theatre group. In his mid-forties, he is fatherly and jocular. Something about his eyes, if not his teeth, reminds me of the comedian Ken Dodd. As a sailor, he's been round the world a few times. Now theatre and singing are his passions, and he's taken a city job so that he can stay in one place and attend regular rehearsals. He sings bass in the chorus confidently enough, as long as there are plenty of other 'fellas' around to support him. He tells me he doesn't know how to contact the power in his voice, which he feels is there beneath the surface 'somewhere'.

In a voice session at the piano, where we explore the range of his voice, I ask him to sing on the words 'How now, brown cow'. This relaxes him, and pleases his sense of humour, and he puts a lot of dramatic expression into each sound, clearly enjoying the exercise and having fun entertaining the rest of the group. He repeats the phrase tone by tone, until he comes to the 'break', or 'changeover' place, between the lower and higher register.

'Sorry,' he says, 'It won't go any further – the cow, I mean. It's come to a ditch.'

'All right, play around in the ditch for a bit,' I suggest, which raises a few ribald comments – but we carry on. 'Let your voice be in the ditch, let it be broken – forget about the cow, let's hear the ditch.'

'The ditch, you mean? You really mean sing like a ditch? I've sung like a drain, but never a ditch.'

Once again, Bob follows the idea with a lot of humour, allowing his voice to crack and croak. 'There's a few frogs down there,' he says, 'that's for sure.'

We are in that 'funny area', where the voice seems to have two, three or even more strands or colours.

'Try and listen to the different strands of sound as you let them out,' I say, 'and then choose to accentuate one, more than the other, like choosing which of the many voices, or frogs, you want to have – and take time to breathe in!'

This engages his imagination even more, and his voice rattles around, note by note, up and down, swooping and soaring, then plunging and crackling within that particular 'ditch', until he settles on a very small but very warm and clear sound.

'Sounds like you've found something interesting in the ditch,' I say, but his humour has given way to a sudden serious concentration. I play a note higher in pitch and he repeats it.

'Is this me? Is this my voice?' he asks, then gestures to me to play another note that he can use to anchor his voice. I love it when a pupil gets so engaged with a newly emerging sound that I am able to adopt my true role – of being merely a guide in the exploration.

I notice that although Bob is using enormous concentration to make this new sound, his whole body stance and face are open and relaxed once this particular and strangely easy tone has emerged. As I play each note, the new sound in his voice develops gaining strength and resonance; it has a warm, beautiful quality that had been completely missing on our first excursion: it is also, to my ears, quite clearly feminine. Bob seems quite entranced by this new quality coming out of his mouth.

'How now, brown cow,' he sings, quipping: 'It's a Jersey cow all right, this one!'

'Forget about the cow,' I say, 'allow yourself to feel the sound for yourself.'

I want to find an image that will help Bob take this new sound as seriously as I sense he really wants to. His sense of comedy is not helping him at the moment. He needs a new image to bring a poetic feeling to the sound, and a word that is easy and pleasurable to sing. A class member suggests that he sing on the word 'Dulcinea'. This is familiar ground: he has recently performed *Man of La Mancha* with his amateur group. The word 'Dulcinea', together with its associations which enable it to touch him, allow Bob to enjoy the new and very musical quality in his voice, as well as to sing into the full circle through his whole body to support each out-breath.

'I never knew I had this kind of voice in me – it's a totally new experience,' he says. And then added, 'It's woman-power; I might have known.'

The resulting warmth, resonance and power is truly astounding, as the uniting of feminine and masculine qualities in the voice often is.

6. LAURA

'Where, oh where, is love?'
Lionel Bart, 'Where is Love?', from *Oliver!*, 1960

Laura is new to singing, and still discovering her voice. In an 'animal aria' exercise she chooses to work with the image of a lynx, working carefully on the movements. Her lynx is stealthy, careful and feline, her eyes watchful and wary. She really does give the illusion of moving through high grass, looking for prey, ready to pounce and yet fearful of being pounced upon, vulnerable yet wild. She adds some sharp feline hissing at some unseen foe as she sings. Once her animal character is clearly established, I ask her to start singing her song – this time using her own singing voice, but still being influenced by the lynx image, and continuing all the time with the lynx movements. The lynx image immediately gives her the right emotional tone for the part and enables her to give a new and authentic dimension to the song. By concentrating on the external characteristics, the inner qualities follow quite simply on the words and melody of the song – Laura can show her own vulnerability and longing from the safety of the image. Now she is able to sing the song while holding on to that inner image and feeling, but without the external movements. It gives her an inner structure, and it does something wonderful, not only to her voice but also to her face – her eyes and mouth become amazingly mobile and expressive.

'Yes,' she says, 'even when I stopped the movements, I could still feel the furry lynx face and eyes, and they seemed to tell me everything I needed to know.'

7. THE RAW LION'S ROAR

'The Rhythm of Life is a powerful beat,
Puts a tingle in your fingers and a tingle in your feet.'

Dorothy Fields, 'The Rhythm of Life',
from *Sweet Charity*, 1969

Ken's throat is a battleground, or has been. His experience of ancient battles long since won or lost gives him a jaw that is clamped, portcullis-like, over any possible unmanly and personal public display of weakness, vulnerability or tears. He has not only a stiff upper lip, but also a jutting and pugnacious chin. No whinging allowed! He is an experienced actor who, like so many, had found little opportunity for training between contracts and performances: he brings with him what could clearly be perceived as 'baggage', full of anger.

In conventional terms, the anger is not evident – he is a co-operative, attentive and willing student. But traces of previously experienced anger are visible nonetheless in the set of his jaw, the coldness in his eyes, the stiffness of his body and the tension in his shoulders. It is audible in the forced and harsh tone of his voice that prevents the full and satisfying expression of his song. The anger has become part of his strategy for confronting tasks that have to be done, and he has evidently decided that 'singing this damn song is one of the tasks, so let's get to it!' He has prepared 'The Rhythm of Life' from the musical *Sweet Charity*. He has sung it through before, but never to his own satisfaction.

'I know there's more to the song, and I know there's more to my voice, if only I can get to it,' he says. Certainly on previous occasions he has always made the song sound too clever, too tough, too cool.

Aggressiveness and anger are both expressions of energy. Ken says he wants to roar; he wants to connect his voice to animal images, but neither his throat nor his jaw will let him. It is as if everything goes back inside: his face gets redder, his eyes bulge – should the lion roar like this, it would definitely get a sore throat!

Only when he allows his jaw to relax; only when he moves his spine: twisting and turning, mobilising lungs and rib cage – only when a spate of deep yawning stretches open his throat and brings tears to his eyes, can he begin to find and release the deep roaring sound he seeks to express, free of his throat. I ask him to repeat the sound, this time on the note I play in the lower register at the piano, then to let the energy of the sound he produces take the pitch upwards. 'But,' I say, 'always come back to the base note at the end of each breath.'

This way, as the pitch gets higher, the roars turn into formidable screeches, piercing through into the higher register. It could have been quite scary.

'Is anyone frightened?' I ask.

'No!' comes the reply from a group used to working with each other. 'More!'

It seems to me that at a certain point the desire to 'sound out anger' gives way to a desire to explore quite new and 'interesting' vocal possibilities, as we have often observed small babies doing. When Ken suddenly realises this, to our delight the roar turns into laughter – deep, rich belly laughs – then in turn the laughs become a rich and rollicking red-wine kind of singing voice, full of guts and vigour. We explore and anchor these new and highly individual vocal qualities up and down the piano, within the range of his song, until Ken feels confident that he is in possession of them. His whole face has changed, as has the colour of his skin. His eyes have softened, his smile and chest have broadened, his shoulders dropped and his movements have become relaxed and fluid.

'Now sing your song – from that source, with that energy – sing it as though drunk with life: sing it like the Lion King himself.'

Once the body starts to sing, the voice begins to move.

8. KATE

'I sing because I'm happy, I sing because I'm free.'
Mahalia Jackson, American gospel singer

Kate wants me to hear the song she is preparing for an audition. She has musical experience, and has often sung in choirs, but says that the experience rarely allows her to really 'feel' the music. She feels she has been protected and prevented from this by holding the music score in front of her and also by being surrounded by other singers. Now she wants to discover what it is like to sing on her own.

She's a friend of mine, so I listen to her right there in her own sitting room. But it is as though she isn't really there – in her imagination she is already onstage, facing the critical gaze of the audition panel. She focuses on a point above my head and sings 'out there' for 'them'. Her two young children tumble about the room, occasionally listening and sometimes singing along, for which they are hushed. This is important, serious stuff.

The song is 'Sunrise, Sunset' from *Fiddler on the Roof* (1964). The old mother sings about her love for her children and her amazement and pride at how they are growing so fast, and of her sadness that she will lose them. Kate shows her lack of confidence by being embarrassed about her own singing – quite without reason. She has a lovely, warm generous voice, and I know she has the ability to carry those qualities into the lower and higher register. She is afraid of not 'getting' the high notes, and fears running out of breath. When she has sung through her song, she makes a face, as if to say, 'not very good, was it?'

There is an ironing-board in the corner of the room, with a pile of her husband's shirts on it. I ask her to sing through the song again, this time existing completely in the room, forgetting about 'them' and singing for herself and for us. I ask her to stand by the ironing board, to do the ironing, and to respond to the children if they come into the room while she is singing. She begins the song again, and from the first phrase it comes to life – it is as though the text has been written for her. Her stiffness leaves her as she turns naturally to look at her children when they distract her, addressing her song to them. The words then start to fit her own sentiments so well that she becomes tearful as she sings.

'Mummy, why are you crying? Don't cry,' says her six-year-old.

'She wants to cry,' I say, 'don't you cry sometimes?'

Kate immediately laughs through her tears.

'Now you see she's laughing – sing the song like that, between tears and laughter; make a mess of it and don't worry about the notes – you can sing the notes: sing the song.'

Whatever tightening there may have been in her throat, the tears dissolve it and Kate carries on singing. She sings through her tears, accepting them and all that dissolving wetness around the eyes. She manages to make a space for them, and they in turn open up a way to her own feeling, and, eventually, happiness. There is no conflict, there is no fighting against the tears, the throat has not become a battleground between body impulses and brain commands; there is acceptance, even relief. And Kate's singing gets better – it fills out and flows, informed with compassion for herself and the story she is singing. She has no trouble whatsoever in singing the top notes when she no longer fears them as impossible targets placed beyond her reach, but sees the notes quite differently as being there to heighten the song's emotional sensibility and enhance its meaning.

9. SAL

'L'amour est un oiseau rebelle.'
[*'Love is a wild untameable bird.'*]
Bizet, 'La Habañera', from *Carmen*, 1875

I haven't met many women who at some point in their singing careers, whether amateur or professional, have not tried to sing or dreamed of singing the role of Carmen, especially the well-known song 'La Habañera'. It's a marvellous song to sing, from every point of view, and one of those songs that never ceases to challenge both the feeling and the imagination. We made the song, together with other scenes from the opera, the focus of one of our workshops. Each participant also had to work on another song appropriate to the Carmen character.

Sal, an actress with no training as a singer, chooses 'Hey Big Spender'. She has no trouble whatsoever in singing the song, and throws in all her acting talent, but 'La Habañera' is another matter.

'I hate this song,' she says. 'I can't sing it how it ought to be sung; now I don't even want to sing it at all!'

This is despite the fact that she has signed up for the workshop to do just that!

'All right,' I say, 'sing "Big Spender" again, then.'

At once, Sal starts to enjoy herself – she loosens up, unwinds, flirts, acts. At once her voice fills with expression, and her body becomes alive and mobile, whereas before she was rigid with fright before the 'classical' number.

'Now sing "La Habañera" like that.'

'But it's the wrong sound.'

'Who says it's the wrong sound?'

'Well, you know – singers, musicians . . . '

'Are you planning to audition for the part at La Scala, Milan?'

'No, of course not. I'm not an opera singer.'

'Well then, just sing it for fun – for what it can give you, for where it can take you. You've worked for days on the words, the melody, the rhythm: trust yourself. And take the 'Big Spender' character out into the woods a bit, get her doing a bit of sorcery to catch those men. Use a few spells.'

Our pianist plays the opening chord and the four magical introductory bars, and Sal begins again with the 'Big Spender' character and voice, plus an element of something new. It works immediately. She starts looking around the group for 'victims' for her Medusa-like charms, and the words and music flow easily, without any hesitation or break.

'Feedback?' I ask the group.

'Hugely enjoyable!'

'Bewitching!'

'Full of life!'

'Total Carmen!'

'Was it beautiful?' I ask Sal.

'No-o, it certainly wasn't beautiful, but it was so much fun – and I *did* it!'

'And did you enjoy singing it this time?'

'Me? I loved it! It's *totally* my song!'

10. EVA SINGS A TANGO

'If I had understood that your kisses held thorns,
and your caresses were of the devil.'

Tango, traditional

Eva stands solid and square, singing, 'full on', a tango song about betrayal in love. She is a dark-haired woman, with a strong stocky physique: young, semi-professional. Good diction and rhythm: she knows her stuff.

'Feedback?'

'Bitter.'

'Business-like.'

'Been there, done that.'

'She's not going back to him, that's for sure.'

And she's not giving much away about Eva yet, I think to myself.

'Let's hear it again, shall we? Can we lower the pitch – you can sing in a deeper range, can't you? We don't have to sing it in this key.'

Our pianist obligingly transposes the chords.

The lower pitch, which is more comfortable for Eva, immediately takes her closer to her own feelings, and gradually we began to hear 'her'.

'Now let's see where we can take it,' I suggest.

The great advantage of developing your singing in a group context is that there are other people around to help you. In this workshop we had a good dancer. I suggest that he take Eva dancing. He holds her close, close enough to take her breath away. She looks a bit worried, but also pleased, and I can see her falsely bright expression softening into something more real and deeply felt. Accompanied by our pianist, she sings as her partner guides her expertly around the floor, his hand pressed into her back. As her concentration focuses more on the dance steps, and on following her partner, so her voice opens out. She no longer has any need to interpret. She sings the words, and the song begins to sing itself. It is magical.

> '*My heart is looking for hope,*
> *Hope is looking for a way*
> *A way to find a dream*
> *Dreams searching for love . . . '*

She sighs and smiles as her partner whirls her about.

'New feedback?'

'Youthful.'

'Vulnerable.'

'Another kind of woman.'

She has lost that sense of weariness, and the hardness that comes from experience, that we have all heard so often before, I thought to myself. This is what had coloured her first rendition: 'I know it all, I have been through it all, I have suffered it all, and you can't hurt me any more.'

'Do you like the feedback?'

'Yes, it's surprising – it's a side of me that I don't often show.'

'So – now you have two ways to sing the song; and maybe there's a third way?'

I ask her, to begin with, to stay with the feeling she has, as though she has been left all alone on the dance floor after everyone has gone home.

'Imagine that the lights are low, the band has stopped playing, but you are still singing to your lover – see what happens.'

Keeping the warm, low, even tone she has found, and the expressive softness, she sings '*Desperation lives inside*', gently and without any of the rage that was there before. The words carry all the meaning, the melody and the fragility in her voice: '*If I had understood that your kisses held thorns, and your caresses were of the devil,*' she sings on her own – and turns, as though still in the dance. She hypnotises us all with the intensity of her feeling, and both she and the song are completely transformed. We could sit there for hours, listening and watching.

> '*It's a pity neither of us can sing.*'
> Charles to Sebastian,
> in Evelyn Waugh, *Brideshead Revisited*, 1945

EPILOGUE
Voice and Soul

'Soul clap its hands and sing . . . '

W.B. Yeats, 'Sailing to Byzantium', 1927

'Soul' is about keeping the inner ear open, about being true to yourself, and about recognising and staying close to the sources of inspiration which nourish your dreams. When we remember that singing is not about getting, but about giving, then we are close to 'soul'. When we sing for the love of singing, for the love of music, for the love of a person or a place: when we sing about something that matters to us, no matter what, we sing with 'soul'.

'Soul' is the sum total of all we are; and most of all, it is that which emanates from us, it is what we give out. This total 'giving out' is what makes 'soul' so exciting in singing. 'Soul' is the essence of ourselves that we are able to pour into every expressive act, no matter how small. 'Soul' means that we are singing from the inside out. It refers to those moments of searching, of the aloneness we need in order to develop, but it doesn't stop there. 'Soul' includes our personality, emotion and energy; our past and present; our belief systems; our imperfections, our strivings, and our struggles. 'Soul' is nothing if it is not invigorating and alive and full of pith and moment, however ordinary the circumstances. Think of people or singers you consider to have 'soul' quality – they are alive, working, struggling, involved and engaged in the present moment, totally dedicated to the person they're with, giving, receiving and empathising: full of generosity, heart, guts and energy.

At this point in our exploration of 'soul' it might be interesting to think about two important characters from Greek mythology who are represented constantly, in many different shapes and forms, in the visual arts and music, and who exert a deep, if unconscious, influence upon us.

DIONYSIUS – THE MANY-VOICED GOD

The first of these is Bacchus, or Dionysius. Dionysius is a god – one of the immortals – and a mover and shaker. His legacy is an integral part of the heritage of rock singing – think of Janis Joplin, Mick Jagger, and others. He is a rousing, carousing god, encouraging people to forget themselves in drunken orgies of wine and song. Dionysius is the inspiration for Carnival and Mardi

Gras. As such, he is often portrayed as leading a procession of people and wild animals, creating disorder and chaos, causing disturbance, breaking rules and engendering panic, tearing down old traditions and making new ones possible – women desert their husbands and families, for instance, to join the frenzied throng dancing and weaving across towns and forests. His followers, possessed by the spirit of demonic singing and dancing, continue until they drop from exhaustion.

Dionysius is sensual and passionate, strong and responsive, his voice reflecting his own state of constant metamorphosis – a child one moment and the devil the next. He unites contradictions and opposites within his persona, such as high and low voices and male and female 'sounds': he has even been known to sing with many voices at once.

'I tell you: one moment he's singing like a woman, crooning,
you know – all seduction and charm, the next he's screeching
like a madman, then he bellows. Yes, that's what I said –
bellows! That man is like an animal, he fascinates me.
So much raw emotion, it's wild. I have to be around him,
but I get scared, but I want to join in and rip and roar and
shriek like he does, he's crazy! He's possessed, yet I guess
he knows exactly what he's doing. He's got beat. And words,
he loves them – he chews them and spews them! Like he's got
the gift of tongues or something, massive, got a voice like
a hurricane...'

ORPHEUS – THE HEAVENLY SINGER

The other important mythological character, Orpheus, does not drive people mad, or lead them anywhere; he stops them in their tracks, enchanting them with his singing and the music of his lyre. He literally charms the birds off the trees. Remember the film *Black Orpheus* (1959)?

He keeps a cool head when everyone around is losing theirs as they dance, drink and follow the crowd. He sings of love, and particularly of the love he holds for Eurydice. According to legend, Eurydice dies, and Orpheus goes to Hades, the underworld, to bring her back to life. He is allowed to do this on one condition – that he must lead her and she must follow, and that he must not look back. As we know, he falters, looks back and loses Eurydice forever. After this, his singing is imbued with great sadness and beauty, and an almost unbearable longing, as he tells of his fruitless attempt to bring his love back to life.

EPILOGUE

'The sound illuminated . . . a pervasive golden sound.
Dancing, it entered the bloodstream. It pulsed and shook
through the mind and soul, moving with each new impossible
cadence deeper than any spoken, written word could
ever reach. People wept, then smiled, their eyes shone l
ong after the singer had stopped. They felt as though
they had been laughing, or loving, or both . . . '

From these two extremes of character we can draw inspiration and set our own compass. Where are you going? What kind of singer do you want to become? The one in the midst of the party, the mover and shaker; or the one who stills, enchants and charms people – or both? The more we allow our whole selves to illuminate our songs and our singing, the more the quality of 'soul' will shine through, to give individuality and humanity to our voices.

Alfred Wolfsohn called the voice, 'the muscle of the soul'. What do muscles do? They stretch, contract and relax. They hold the body together and allow it to dance, and to sing.

BIBLIOGRAPHY

Attenborough, David, *The Life of Birds,* London: BBC Books, 1998

Balk, H. Wesley, *The Radiant Performer,* Minneapolis: University of Minnesota Press, 1991

Chatwin, Bruce, *The Songlines,* London: Jonathan Cape, 1987

Cook, Nicolas, *Music: a Very Short Introduction,* Oxford: Oxford University Press, 1998

Dewhurst-Maddock, Olivea, *The Book of Sound Therapy: Heal Yourself with Music and Voice,* London: Gaia, 1993

Falkner, Sir Keith (ed.), *Voice,* Yehudi Menuhin Music Guides, London: Kahn and Averill, 1994

Feldenkrais, Moshe, *The Elusive Obvious, or Basic Feldenkrais,* Cupertino: Meta, 1981

Fischer, Jean M.O. (ed.), *The Philosopher's Stone: Diaries of Lessons with F. Matthias Alexander,* London: Mouritz, 1998

Fisher, Hilda B., *Voice and Articulation,* Boston: Houghton Mifflin, 1966

Ginsbourger, Marianne, *La Voix de L'Inoui,* Barret-sur-Meouge: Souffle d'Or, 1997

Goodchild, Chloë, *The Naked Voice: Journey to the Source of Sound,* London: Rider, 1993

Hampton and Acker, *The Vocal Vision,* New York: Applause Books, 1992

Hemsley, Thomas, *Singing & Imagination: a Human Approach to a Great Musical Tradition,* Oxford: Oxford University Press, 1998

Hewitt, Graham, *How to Sing,* London: Elm Tree Books/ EMI Music Publishing, 1978

Hill, David; Ash, Elizabeth & Parfitt, Hilary, *Giving Voice: a Handbook for Choir Directors and Trainers,* Rattlesden: Kevin Mayhew, 1995

Hollingworth, Julie, *Between the Lines: Understanding Music Theory,* Hereford: Julie Hollingworth, 1993

Houseman, Barbara, *Finding Your Voice,* London & New York: Nick Hern Books & Routledge, 2002

Kagen, Sergius, *On Studying Singing,* New York: Dover Publications, 1960

Keyes, Laurel Elisabeth, *Toning: The Creative Power of the Voice,* Los Angeles: De Vorss & Co., 1973

Laine, Cleo, *You Can Sing if You Want To,* London: Victor Gollancz, 1997

Latham, Alison (ed.), *The Oxford Companion to Music,* Oxford: Oxford UP, 2002

Quignard, Pascal, *La Leçon de Musique,* Paris: Hachette, 1987

Salaman, Esther, *Unlocking Your Voice: Freedom to Sing,* London: Victor Gollancz, 1989

Seldon, Philip, and Sherman, Robert, *The Complete Idiot's Guide to Classical Music,* New York: Alpha Books, 1997

Trevelyan, Sir George, *Magic Casements: The Use of Poetry in the Expanding of Consciousness,* London: Coventure, 1980

Wilson, Pat, *The Singing Voice: An Owner's Manual,* London & Sydney: Nick Hern Books and Currency Press, 1997

INDEX OF EXERCISES